Math Mammoth
Grade 6-B Worktext

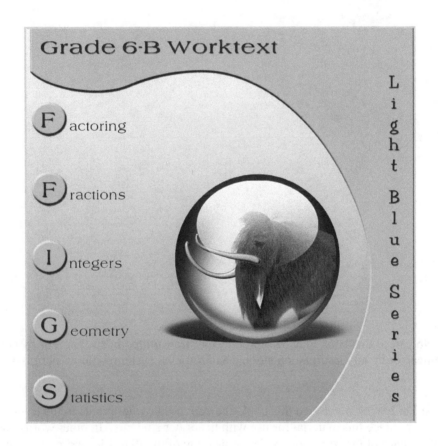

By Maria Miller

Contents

Chapter 9: Geometry

Chapter 10: Statistics

Foreword

Math Mammoth Grade 6 comprises a complete math curriculum for the sixth grade mathematics studies. The curriculum meets and exceeds the Common Core standards.

In sixth grade, we have quite a few topics to study. Some of them, such as fractions and decimals, students are familiar with, but many others are introduced for the first time (e.g. exponents, ratios, percent, integers). The main areas of study in Math Mammoth Grade 6 are:

- An introduction to several algebraic concepts, such as exponents, expressions, and equations;
- Rational numbers: fractions, decimals, and percents;
- Ratios, rates, and problem solving using bar models;
- Geometry: area, volume, and surface area;
- Integers and graphing;
- Statistics: students learn to describe distributions using measures of center and variability.

This book, 6-B, covers number theory topics (chapter 6), fractions (chapter 7), integers (chapter 8), geometry (chapter 9), and statistics (chapter 10). The rest of the topics are covered in the 6-A worktext.

Some important points to keep in mind when using the curriculum:

- The two books (parts A and B) are like a "framework", but you still have a lot of liberty in planning your child's studies. For the most part, the chapters in the 6th grade curriculum don't have to be studied in the order presented, but you can choose, for example, to study integers before decimals, or statistics right after ratios.

  Math Mammoth is mastery-based, which means it concentrates on a few major topics at a time, in order to study them in depth. However, you can still use it in a *spiral* manner, if you prefer. Simply have your child study in 2-3 chapters simultaneously. This type of flexible use of the curriculum enables you to truly individualize the instruction for your child.

- Don't automatically assign all the exercises. Use your judgment, trying to assign just enough for your child's needs. You can use the skipped exercises later for review. For most children, I recommend to start out by assigning about half of the available exercises. Adjust as necessary.

- For review, the curriculum includes a worksheet maker (Internet access required), mixed review lessons, additional cumulative review lessons, and the word problems continually require usage of past concepts. Please see more information about review (and other topics) in the FAQ at
  https://www.mathmammoth.com/faq-lightblue.php

I heartily recommend that you view the full user guide for your grade level, available at
https://www.mathmammoth.com/userguides/

Lastly, you can find free videos matched to the curriculum at https://www.mathmammoth.com/videos/

I wish you success in teaching math!
Maria Miller, the author

Chapter 6: Prime Factorization, GCF, and LCM
Introduction

The topics of this chapter belong to a branch of mathematics known as *number theory*. Number theory has to do with the study of whole numbers and their special properties. In this chapter, we review prime factorization and study the greatest common factor (GCF) and the least common multiple (LCM).

The main application of factoring and the greatest common factor in arithmetic is in simplifying fractions, so that is why I have included a lesson on that topic. However, it is not absolutely necessary to use the GCF when simplifying fractions, and the lesson emphasizes that fact.

The concepts of factoring and the GCF are important to understand because they will be carried over into algebra, where students will factor polynomials. In this chapter, we lay the groundwork for that by using the GCF to factor simple sums, such as $27 + 45$. For example, a sum like $27 + 45$ factors into $9(3 + 5)$.

Similarly, the main use for the least common multiple in arithmetic is in finding the smallest common denominator for adding fractions, and we study that topic in this chapter in connection with the LCM.

Primes are fascinating "creatures," and you can let students read more about them by accessing the Internet resources listed below. The really important, but far more advanced, application of prime numbers is in cryptography. Some students might be interested in reading additional material on that subject—please see the list below for Internet resources.

Keep in mind that the specific lessons in the chapter can take several days to finish. They are not "daily lessons." Instead, use the general guideline that sixth graders should finish about 2 pages daily or 9-10 pages a week in order to finish the curriculum in about 40 weeks. Also, I recommend not assigning all the exercises by default, but that you use your judgment, and strive to vary the number of assigned exercises according to the student's needs.

Please see the user guide at https://www.mathmammoth.com/userguides/ for more guidance on using and pacing the curriculum.

You can find some free videos for the topics of this chapter at https://www.mathmammoth.com/videos/ (choose 6th grade).

The Lessons in Chapter 6

Helpful Resources on the Internet

PRIMES

Sieve of Eratosthenes
Explore the sieve of Eratosthenes with this virtual online chart.
http://www.visnos.com/demos/sieve-of-eratosthenes

Sieve of Eratosthenes till 400
Click on any number and all its proper multiples will be removed from the table. Requires java.
http://www.hbmeyer.de/eratosiv.htm

Primes, Factors and Divisibility – Explorer at CountOn.org
Lessons explaining divisibility tests, primes, and factors.
https://web.archive.org/web/20180319072651/http://www.counton.org/explorer/primes/

Prime Number Calculator
This calculator tests to see if a number is a prime, and tells you its smallest divisor if it is not a prime.
http://www.basic-mathematics.com/prime-number-calculator.html

Prime Numbers as Building Blocks – Euclid's Greatest Discovery
A short video about the fundamental theorem of arithmetic: that each composite number has a unique prime factorization.
http://www.youtube.com/watch?v=5kl28hmhin0

The Prime Pages
Learn more about primes on this site: the largest known primes, finding primes, how many there are, and more.
http://primes.utm.edu/

Primality of 1
Discussing whether 1 should or should not be counted as a prime number.
http://en.wikipedia.org/wiki/Prime_number#Primality_of_one

http://primefan.tripod.com/Prime1ProCon.html

PRIME FACTORIZATION

Factorization Forest
For each number you factorize, you will get to grow a tree in your forest! Choose from 6 different trees.
http://mrnussbaum.com/forest/

Factor Trees at Math Playground
Factor numbers to their prime factors using an interactive factor tree, or find the GCF and LCM of numbers.
http://www.mathplayground.com/factortrees.html

MathGoodies Interactive Factor Tree Game
Type in a missing number from the factor tree, and the program will find the other factor and continue drawing the tree as needed.
http://www.mathgoodies.com/factors/prime_factors.html

Free Worksheets for Prime Factorization
Generate free, printable worksheets for prime factorization or for finding all the factors of a given number. Customize the worksheets in various ways (difficulty level, spacing, font size, number of problems.)
http://www.homeschoolmath.net/worksheets/factoring.php

Multiplying Fractions with Cross-Canceling
This fraction worksheet is great for working on multiplying fractions with cross-canceling. The problems may be selected for four different degrees of difficulty.
http://www.math-aids.com/Fractions/Multiplying_Fractions_Cross_Cancel.html

The Cryptoclub. Using Mathematics to Make and Break Secret Codes (book)
Cryptoclub kids strive to break the codes of secret messages, and at the same time learn more and more about encrypting and decrypting. There are problems to solve at the end of each chapter, tips, and historical information on how cryptography has been used over the centuries.
http://www.amazon.com/gp/product/156881223X?tag=mathmammoth-20

FACTORS (FOR REVIEW)

Product Game
The players choose factors and the product of those gets colored in on the game board. The player who gets four products in a row wins. You can play against the computer or with a friend. This game can easily be adapted to be played offline, with paper and colored pencils.
http://illuminations.nctm.org/Activity.aspx?id=4213

Sliding Tile Factorization Game
Slide a number over another number to capture it, if it is a factor of the original number. Number 1 is only supposed to be used to capture a prime number.
http://www.visualmathlearning.com/Games/sliding_factors.html

Connect 4 Factors Game
Practice factors with this interactive game. It can be played by one or two players.
http://www.transum.org/Software/Game/Connect4/

GREATEST COMMON FACTOR AND LEAST COMMON MULTIPLE

Fruit Shoot—Greatest Common Factor
Shoot the fruit that has the greatest common factor of two given numbers. Three levels and two different speeds.
http://www.sheppardsoftware.com/mathgames/fractions/GreatestCommonFactor.htm

Fruit Shoot—Least Common Multiple
Shoot the fruit that has the least common multiple of two given numbers. Three levels and two different speeds.
http://www.sheppardsoftware.com/mathgames/fractions/LeastCommonMultiple.htm

Factors and Multiples Jeopardy Game
A jeopardy game where the questions have to do with factors, multiples, prime factorization, GCF, and LCM.
http://www.math-play.com/Factors-and-Multiples-Jeopardy/Factors-and-Multiples-Jeopardy.html

Factors, LCM, and GCF: Activity from Math Playground
Choose "Find the prime factorization of two numbers, GCF, and LCM." First, you find the prime factorization of two different numbers, using the factor tree. Once that is done, the activity shows you a Venn diagram. Drag the factors of the two numbers into the correct areas, then figure out their GFC and LCM.
http://www.mathplayground.com/factortrees.html

Least Common Multiple
A short illustrated lesson about least common multiples. Scroll to the bottom of the page to find questions that practice the topic.
https://www.mathsisfun.com/least-common-multiple.html

Factors Millionaire Game
A millionaire game where the questions have to do with factors, prime numbers, and the greatest common factor.
http://www.math-play.com/Factors-Millionaire/Factors-Millionaire.html

Greatest Common Factor at ThatQuiz.org
10-question quiz, not timed, difficulty level 5 (medium). You can also change the parameters to your liking.
http://www.thatquiz.org/tq-r/?-j2-l5-p0

GCF and LCM Quiz
10-question quiz, not timed, difficulty level 5 (medium). You can also change the parameters to your liking.
http://www.thatquiz.org/tq-r/?-j4-l5-p0

Math Problems with LCM & GCF
A quiz of 10 word problems involving the usage of the greatest common factor and the least common multiple.
http://www.funtrivia.com/playquiz/quiz2715661f17598.html

LCM and GCF Word Problems
Solve word problems where you either need to find the LCM or the GCF in this interactive exercise.
https://www.khanacademy.org/math/on-sixth-grade-math/on-number-sense-numeration/on-properties-numbers/e/gcf-and-lcm-word-problems

Sketch's World! - Greatest Common Factor (GCF)
Help Sketch get away from the dreaded erasers by giving the correct answers to the questions about the greatest common factor.
http://www.fun4thebrain.com/beyondfacts/gcfsketch.html

Snowball Fight!
Multiple-choice questions on the LCM of two numbers. When you click a right answer, the game throws a snowball for you.
http://www.fun4thebrain.com/beyondfacts/lcmsnowball.html

Pyramid Math
This includes games for GCF, LCM, exponents, and square roots. The question to solve appears on the right, under "example." Choose the triangular tile with the correct answer, and drag it to the solution vase. Includes easy and hard levels, timed and non-timed versions.
http://www.mathnook.com/math/pyramidmath.html

Free Workheets for Greatest Common Factor and Least Common Multiple
Generate free, printable worksheets for GCF and LCM. Customize the worksheets in various ways (choose number range, font size, etc.)
http://www.homeschoolmath.net/worksheets/GCF_LCM.php

FACTORING SUMS

Rewriting Expressions as Multiples of a Sum
Downloadable 12-problem worksheets to practice rewriting expressions as multiples of a sum.
http://www.commoncoresheets.com/SortedByGrade.php?Sorted=6ns4

Factor with the Distributive Property
Practice applying the distributive property to factor numerical expressions (no variables).
https://www.khanacademy.org/math/on-sixth-grade-math/on-number-sense-numeration/on-properties-numbers/e/distributive_property

The Sieve of Eratosthenes and Prime Factorization

To find all the prime numbers less than 100 we can use the *sieve of Eratosthenes*.

1. Cross out 1, as it is not considered a prime.
2. Cross out all the even numbers except 2.
3. Cross out all the multiples of 3 except 3.
4. You do not have to check multiples of 4. Why?
5. Cross out all the multiples of 5 except 5.
6. You do not have to check multiples of 6. Why?
7. Cross out all the multiples of 7 except 7.
8. You do not have to check multiples of 8 or 9 or 10.
9. The numbers left are **primes**. The numbers you crossed out are **composite numbers**.

1̶	2	3	4̶	5	6̶	7	8̶	9	10
11	12	13	14	15	16	17	18	19	20
21	22	23	24	25	26	27	28	29	30
31	32	33	34	35	36	37	38	39	40
41	42	43	44	45	46	47	48	49	50
51	52	53	54	55	56	57	58	59	60
61	62	63	64	65	66	67	68	69	70
71	72	73	74	75	76	77	78	79	80
81	82	83	84	85	86	87	88	89	90
91	92	93	94	95	96	97	98	99	100

List the primes you found: 2, 3, 5, 7,
_____

Why do you not have to check numbers that are bigger than 10? Let's think about multiples of 11. The following multiples of 11 have already been crossed out: 2×11, 3×11, 4×11, 5×11, 6×11, 7×11, 8×11, and 9×11. The multiples of 11 that have not been crossed out are 10×11 and onward... but they are not on our chart! Similarly, the multiples of 13 that are less than 100 are 2×13, 3×13, ..., 7×13, and all of those have already been crossed out when you crossed out multiples of 2, 3, 5, and 7.

Use the various divisibility tests when building a factor tree for a composite number.

135
/ \
5 × ?

$$\begin{array}{r} 27 \\ 5\overline{)135} \\ -10 \\ \hline 35 \\ -35 \\ \hline 0 \end{array}$$

135
/ \
5 × 27
/ \
3 × 9
/ \
3 × **3**

We start out by noticing that 135 is **divisible by 5.** From long division, we know that $135 = 5 \times 27$. The final factorization is $135 = 3 \times 3 \times 3 \times 5$ or $3^3 \times 5$.

441
/ \
9 × ?

$$\begin{array}{r} 49 \\ 9\overline{)441} \\ -36 \\ \hline 81 \\ -81 \\ \hline 0 \end{array}$$

441
/ \
9 × 49
/ \ / \
3 × **3** × **7** × **7**

Adding the digits of 441, we get 9, so it is **divisible by 9.** We divide to get $441 = 9 \times 49$. The end result is $441 = 3 \times 3 \times 7 \times 7$ or $3^2 \times 7^2$.

912
/ \
4 × ?

$$\begin{array}{r} 228 \\ 4\overline{)912} \\ -8 \\ \hline 11 \\ -8 \\ \hline 32 \\ -32 \\ \hline 0 \end{array}$$

The last two digits of 912 are "12" so it is **divisible by 4.**

912
/ \
4 × 228
/ \ / \
$2 \times 2 \times 4 \times 57$

228, too, is **divisible by 4** (its last digits are "28").

912
/ \
4 × 228
/ \ / \
2 × **2** × 4 × 57
/ \ / \
2 × **2** × **3** × **19**

Lastly, 57 is 3×19. The prime factorization of 912 is $2^4 \times 3 \times 19$.

1. Find the prime factorization of these composite numbers. Use a notebook for long divisions.

a. 124
 	
  /   \\
2 × ___
     / \\
	b. 260
	
	   / \\
	10 × ___
	  / \\ / \\
		c. 96
		
		  / \\
		3 × ___
		      / \\

d. 90	**e.** 165	**f.** 95
g. 80	**h.** 240	**i.** 272
j. 76	**k.** 126	**l.** 104

2. Find the prime factorization of these composite numbers.

a. 196	b. 380	c. 336
d. 306	e. 116	f. 720
g. 675	h. 990	i. 945

Puzzle Corner Find all the primes between 0 and 200. Use the sieve of Eratosthenes again (you need to make a grid in your notebook).

This time, you need to cross out 1, and then every even number except 2, every multiple of 3 except 3, every multiple of 5 except 5, every multiple of 7 except 7, every multiple of 11 except 11, and every multiple of 13 except 13.

Using Factoring When Simplifying Fractions

On this page, we will review simplifying fractions. Let your teacher decide if you can skip this page.

You are used to seeing the process of **simplifying fractions** like this: →

In simplifying fractions, we divide both the numerator and the denominator by the same number. The fraction becomes *simpler*, which means that the numerator and the denominator are now *smaller* numbers than they were before.

These slices have been joined together in threes.

$$\xrightarrow{\div 3}$$
$$\frac{6}{9} = \frac{2}{3}$$
$$\xleftarrow{\div 3}$$

However, this does NOT change the actual value of the fraction. It is the "same amount of pie" as it was before. It is just cut differently.

We can simplify a fraction only if its numerator and denominator are divisible by the same number:

We *can* simplify $\frac{25}{65}$ because both 25 and 65 are divisible by 5: →

We *cannot* simplify $\frac{11}{20}$ because 11 and 20 do not have any common divisors except 1.

$$\xrightarrow{\div 5}$$
$$\frac{25}{65} = \frac{5}{13}$$
$$\xleftarrow{\div 5}$$

You can simplify in multiple steps. Just start somewhere, using the divisibility tests. The goal is to simplify the fraction to **lowest terms,** where the numerator and the denominator have no common factors.

$$\frac{42}{60} \xrightarrow{\div 2} = \frac{21}{30} \xrightarrow{\div 3} = \frac{7}{10}$$

$$\frac{180}{780} \xrightarrow{\div 10} = \frac{18}{78} \xrightarrow{\div 2} = \frac{9}{39} \xrightarrow{\div 3} = \frac{3}{13}$$

1. Simplify the fractions to the lowest terms, if possible.

a. $\frac{12}{36}$	**b.** $\frac{45}{55}$	**c.** $\frac{15}{23}$	**d.** $\frac{13}{6}$
e. $\frac{15}{21}$	**f.** $\frac{19}{15}$	**g.** $\frac{17}{24}$	**h.** $\frac{24}{30}$

2. Simplify the fractions. Use your knowledge of divisibility.

a. $\frac{95}{100}$	**b.** $\frac{66}{82}$	**c.** $\frac{69}{99}$
d. $\frac{120}{600}$	**e.** $\frac{38}{52}$	**f.** $\frac{72}{84}$

3. Simplify the fractions. Write the simplified numerator above and the simplified denominator below the old ones.

a. $\dfrac{14}{16}$	**b.** $\dfrac{33}{27}$	**c.** $\dfrac{12}{26}$	**d.** $\dfrac{9}{33}$	**e.** $\dfrac{42}{28}$

Using factoring when simplifying

Carefully study the example on the right where we factor 96/144.

$$\frac{96}{144} = \frac{\overset{2}{\cancel{8}} \times \overset{1}{\cancel{12}}}{\underset{3}{\cancel{12}} \times \underset{1}{\cancel{12}}} = \frac{2}{3}$$

- First we factor (write) 96 as 8 × 12, and 144 as 12 × 12.

- Then we simplify in two steps:

  1. 8 and 12 are both divisible by 4, so they simplify into 2 and 3.

  2. 12 and 12 are divisible by 12, so they simplify into 1 and 1. Essentially, they cancel each other out.

For comparison, the "old" way looks like this:

Let's study some more examples. (Remember that they don't show the number that you divide by.)	$\dfrac{42}{105} = \dfrac{\overset{1}{\cancel{7}} \times \overset{2}{\cancel{6}}}{\underset{5}{\cancel{35}} \times \underset{1}{\cancel{3}}} = \dfrac{2}{5}$	$\dfrac{45}{150} = \dfrac{\overset{3}{\cancel{9}} \times \overset{1}{\cancel{5}}}{\underset{10}{\cancel{30}} \times \underset{1}{\cancel{5}}} = \dfrac{3}{10}$

4. The numerator and the denominator have already been factored in some problems. Your task is to simplify.

a. $\dfrac{56}{84} = \dfrac{7 \times 8}{21 \times 4} =$	**b.** $\dfrac{54}{144} = \dfrac{6 \times 9}{12 \times 12} =$	**c.** $\dfrac{120}{72} = \dfrac{10 \times \boxed{}}{\boxed{} \times 9} =$
d. $\dfrac{80}{48} = \dfrac{\boxed{} \times 8}{\boxed{} \times 8} =$	**e.** $\dfrac{36}{90} = \dfrac{\quad\quad}{\quad\quad} =$	**f.** $\dfrac{28}{140} = \dfrac{\quad\quad}{\quad\quad} =$

Simplify "criss-cross"

These examples are from the previous page. This time the 45 in the numerator has been written as 5 × 9 instead of 9 × 5. We can cancel out the 5 from the numerator with the 5 from the denominator (we simplify criss-cross).

$$\frac{45}{150} = \frac{\overset{1}{\cancel{5}} \times \overset{3}{\cancel{9}}}{\underset{10}{\cancel{30}} \times \underset{1}{\cancel{5}}} = \frac{3}{10}$$

Also, we can simplify the 9 in the numerator and the 30 in the denominator criss-cross. The other example (simplifying 42/105) is similar.

This same concept can be applied to make multiplying fractions easier.

$$\frac{42}{105} = \frac{\overset{1}{\cancel{7}} \times \overset{2}{\cancel{6}}}{\underset{1}{\cancel{3}} \times \underset{5}{\cancel{35}}} = \frac{2}{5}$$

5. Simplify.

a. $\dfrac{14}{84} = \dfrac{2 \times 7}{21 \times 4} =$	**b.** $\dfrac{54}{150} = \dfrac{9 \times \boxed{}}{10 \times \boxed{}} =$	**c.** $\dfrac{138}{36} = \dfrac{2 \times \boxed{}}{\boxed{} \times 4} =$
d. $\dfrac{27}{20} \times \dfrac{10}{21} =$	**e.** $\dfrac{75}{90} = \dfrac{}{} =$	**f.** $\dfrac{48}{45} \times \dfrac{55}{64} =$

In this example, the simplification is done in two steps. In the first step, 12 and 2 are divided by 2, leaving 6 and 1. In the second step, 6 and 69 are divided by 3, leaving 2 and 23.

$$\frac{48}{138} = \frac{\overset{6}{\cancel{12}} \times 4}{\underset{1}{\cancel{2}} \times 69} = \frac{\overset{2}{\cancel{6}} \times 4}{1 \times \underset{23}{\cancel{69}}} = \frac{8}{23}$$

These two steps can also be done without rewriting the expression. The 6 and 69 are divided by 3 as before. This time we simply did not rewrite the expression in between but just continued on with the numbers 6 and 69 that were already written there.

$$\frac{48}{138} = \frac{\overset{\overset{2}{\cancel{6}}}{\cancel{12}} \times 4}{\underset{1}{\cancel{2}} \times \underset{23}{\cancel{69}}} = \frac{8}{23}$$

If this looks too confusing, you do not have to write it in such a compact manner. You can rewrite the expression before simplifying it some more.

6. Simplify the fractions to lowest terms, or simplify before you multiply the fractions.

a. $\dfrac{88}{100}$	**b.** $\dfrac{84}{102}$	**c.** $\dfrac{85}{105}$
d. $\dfrac{8}{5} \times \dfrac{8}{20} =$	**e.** $\dfrac{72}{120}$	**f.** $\dfrac{104}{240}$
g. $\dfrac{35}{98}$	**h.** $\dfrac{5}{7} \times \dfrac{17}{15} =$	**i.** $\dfrac{72}{112}$

The Greatest Common Factor (GCF)

Let's take two whole numbers. We can then list all the <u>factors</u> of each number, and then find the factors that are <u>common</u> in both lists. Lastly, we can choose the <u>greatest</u> or largest among those "common factors." That is the **greatest common factor** of the two numbers. The term itself really tells you what it means!

Example 1. Find the greatest common factor of 18 and 30.

<u>The factors of 18:</u> 1, 2, 3, 6, 9, and 18.
<u>The factors of 30:</u> 1, 2, 3, 5, 6, 10, 15, and 30.

Their <u>common</u> factors are 1, 2, 3, and 6. The <u>greatest</u> common factor is 6.

Here is a **method to find all the factors of a given number**.

Example 2. Find the factors (divisors) of 36.

We check if 36 is divisible by 1, 2, 3, 4, 5, and so on. Each time we find a divisor, we write down *two* factors.

- 36 is divisible by 1. We write <u>$36 = 1 \cdot 36$</u>, and that equation gives us two factors of 36: both the smallest (**1**) and the largest (**36**).

- Next, 36 is also divisible by 2. We write <u>$36 = 2 \cdot 18$</u>, and that equation gives us two more factors of 36: the second smallest (**2**) and the second largest (**18**).

- Next, 36 is divisible by 3. We write <u>$36 = 3 \cdot 12$</u>, and now we have found the third smallest factor (**3**) and the third largest factor (**12**).

- Next, 36 is divisible by 4. We write <u>$36 = 4 \cdot 9$</u>, and we have found the fourth smallest factor (**4**) and the fourth largest factor (**9**).

- Finally, 36 is divisible by 6. We write <u>$36 = 6 \cdot 6$</u>, and we have found the fifth smallest factor (**6**) which is also the fifth largest factor.

We know that we are done because the list of factors from the "small" end (1, 2, 3, 4, 6) has met the list of factors from the "large" end (36, 18, 12, 9, 6).

Therefore, all of the factors of 36 are: 1, 2, 3, 4, 6, 9, 12, 18, and 36.

---

1. List all of the factors of the given numbers.

a. 48	**b.** 60
c. 42	**d.** 99

2. Find the greatest common factor of the given numbers. Your work above will help!

a. 48 and 60	**b.** 42 and 48	**c.** 42 and 60	**d.** 99 and 60

3. List all of the factors of the given numbers.

a. 44	b. 66
c. 28	d. 56
e. 100	f. 45

4. Find the greatest common factor of the given numbers. Your work above will help!

a. 44 and 66	b. 100 and 28	c. 45 and 100	d. 45 and 66
e. 28 and 44	f. 56 and 28	g. 56 and 100	h. 45 and 28

Example 3. What is the greatest common factor useful for?

It can be used to simplify fractions. For example, let's say you know that the GCF of 66 and 84 is 6. Then, to simplify the fraction 66/84 to lowest terms, you divide both the numerator and the denominator by 6. →

However, it is *not* necessary to use the GCF when simplifying fractions. You can always simplify in several steps. See the example at the right. →

Or, you can *simplify by factoring*, like we did in the previous lesson:

$$\frac{66}{84} = \frac{6 \cdot 11}{7 \cdot 6 \cdot 2} = \frac{11}{14}.$$

In fact, these other methods might be quicker than using the GCF.

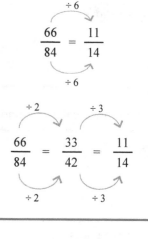

---

5. Simplify these fractions, if possible. Your work in the previous exercises can help!

a. $\dfrac{48}{66}$ b. $\dfrac{42}{44}$ c. $\dfrac{42}{48}$ d. $\dfrac{99}{60}$

e. $\dfrac{48}{100}$ f. $\dfrac{100}{99}$ g. $\dfrac{56}{28}$ h. $\dfrac{44}{99}$

17

Using prime factorization to find the greatest common factor (optional)

Another, more efficient way to find the GCF of two or more numbers is to use the prime factorizations of the numbers to find *all* of the common prime factors. The product of those common prime factors forms the GCF.

Example 4. Find the GCF of 48 and 84.

The prime factorizations are: $48 = 2 \cdot 2 \cdot 2 \cdot 2 \cdot 3$ and $84 = 2 \cdot 2 \cdot 3 \cdot 7$.

We see that the common prime factors are 2 and 2 and 3. Therefore, the GCF is $2 \cdot 2 \cdot 3 = 12$.

Example 5. Find the GCF of 75, 105, and 125.

The prime factorizations are: $75 = 3 \cdot 5 \cdot 5$, $105 = 3 \cdot 5 \cdot 7$, and $150 = 2 \cdot 3 \cdot 5 \cdot 5$.

The common prime factors for all of them are 3 and 5. Therefore, the GCF of these three numbers is $3 \cdot 5 = 15$.

6. Find the greatest common factor of the numbers.

a. 120 and 66	**b.** 36 and 136
c. 98 and 76	**d.** 132 and 72
e. 45 and 76	**f.** 64 and 120

7. Find the greatest common factor of the given numbers.

a. 75, 25, and 90	**b.** 54, 36, and 40
c. 18, 24, and 36	**d.** 72, 60, and 48

Find the greatest common factor of 187 and 264.

Puzzle Corner

Factoring Sums

1. You have seen these before! Write two different expressions for the total area, thinking of: (1) the area of the big rectangle as a whole and (2) the sum of the areas of the two small rectangles.

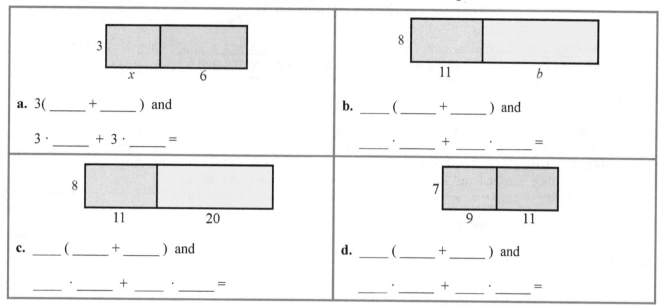

a. 3(_____ + _____) and

    3 · _____ + 3 · _____ =

b. _____ (_____ + _____) and

    _____ · _____ + _____ · _____ =

c. _____ (_____ + _____) and

    _____ · _____ + _____ · _____ =

d. _____ (_____ + _____) and

    _____ · _____ + _____ · _____ =

2. List the length and width of all of the possible rectangles that have an area of 30 square centimeters and sides that are an even (whole) number of centimeters long. The first one would be 1 cm × 30 cm, and the second 2 cm × 15 cm.

3. List the length and width of all of the possible rectangles that have an area of 40 square centimeters and sides that are an even number of centimeters long. The first one would be 1 cm × 40 cm.

4. Build a big rectangle out of two smaller ones like in exercise #1. Choose one rectangle from exercise #2 and one from #3 that each have one side that is the same length. In the grid at the right, sketch the two rectangles that you chose side by side, touching so that they share the side that is the same length. Your sketch should look like the figures in exercise #1.

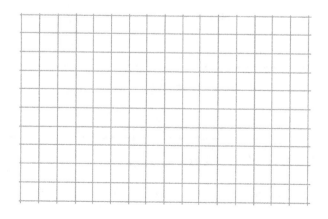

5. Can you find another answer to exercise 4?

Another usage for the GCF is to factor expressions. **Factoring an expression** means writing it as a product (a multiplication).

Example 1. We can easily write the sum $54 + 27$ as multiplication, once we notice that both 54 and 27 have the factor 9. So, $54 + 27$ is $9 \cdot 6 + 9 \cdot 3$. Now, using the distributive property "backwards," we write

$$9 \cdot 6 + 9 \cdot 3 = 9(6 + 3)$$

We have now <u>factored</u> the original sum. This means we have <u>written it as a multiplication</u>. This time we have two factors: the first factor is 9, and the second factor is actually a *sum*: the sum $6 + 3$.

Example 2. Write the sum $92 + 56$ as a multiplication, using the greatest common factor of 92 and 56.

The GCF of 92 and 56 is 4. Therefore, we write $92 + 56 = 4 \cdot 23 + 4 \cdot 14 = 4(23 + 14)$.

Example 3. You have also factored expressions such as $72x + 16$ using the distributive property "backwards." Notice, the GCF of 72 and 16 is 8. We can write $72x + 16$ as $8(9x + 2)$.

6. First find the GCF of the numbers. Then factor the expressions using the GCF.

a. GCF of 18 and 12 is 6

   $18 + 12 =$ 6 $\cdot 3 +$ 6 $\cdot 2 =$ 6 (____ + ____)

b. GCF of 6 and 10 is ____

   $6 + 10 =$ ____ $\cdot$ ____ $+$ ____ $\cdot$ ____ $=$ ____ (____ + ____)

c. GCF of 22 and 11 is ____

   $22 + 11 =$ ____ $\cdot$ ____ $+$ ____ $\cdot$ ____ $=$ ____ (____ + ____)

d. GCF of 15 and 21 is _____

   $15 + 21 =$ ____ $\cdot$ ____ $+$ ____ $\cdot$ ____ $=$ ____ (____ + ____)

e. GCF of 25 and 35 is _____

   $25 + 35 =$ ____ (____ + ____)

f. GCF of 72 and 86 is _____

   $72 + 86 =$ ____ (____ + ____)

g. GCF of 96 and 40 is _____

   $96 + 40 =$ ____ (____ + ____)

h. GCF of 39 and 81 is _____

   $39 + 81 =$ ____ (____ + ____)

7. **a.** Express the sum $32 + 40$ as a product (multiplication).

    b. Draw two rectangles, side by side, to represent the product you wrote.

8. Draw two rectangles, side by side, to represent the sum $30 + 25$.

9. Draw three rectangles, side by side, to represent the sum $42 + 24 + 30$.

10. You need to build a rectangular animal pen that has an area of 45 m^2.
    If the lengths of the sides need to be in whole meters, what are the options?

11. **a.** List a pair of numbers whose greatest common factor is 1.

    b. List two more pairs of numbers whose greatest common factor is 1.

12. Write these sums as a product (multiplication) of their GCF and another sum.

a. The GCF of 15 and 5 is _____	**b.** The GCF of 18 and 30 is _____
$15x + 5 =$ ____ (____ + ____)	$18x + 30 =$ ____ (____ + ____)
c. The GCF of 72 and 54 is _____	**d.** The GCF of 100 and 90 is _____
$72a + 54b =$ ____ (____ + ____)	$100y + 90x =$ ____ (____ + ____)

> **a.** List two numbers whose greatest common factor is 13.
>
> **b.** List two numbers whose greatest common factor is 51.
>
> *Puzzle Corner*

The Least Common Multiple (LCM)

A **multiple** of a whole number n is any of the numbers n, $2n$, $3n$, $4n$, $5n$, and so on. In other words, a whole number times the number n is a multiple of n.

Example 1. The multiples of 9 are 9, 18, 27, 36, 45, 54, 63, and so on.

When we have two or more whole numbers, we can find their **least common multiple**.

As in the case of the greatest common factor, the term "least common multiple" itself tells us what it is! Read it again: least common multiple. All we need to do (in principle) is to find the multiples of the numbers, then find the common multiples, and lastly choose the one that is the least, or the smallest.

Example 2. Find the least common multiple of 5 and 8.

- The multiples of 5 are: 5, 10, 15, 20, 25, 30, 35, <u>40</u>, 45, 50, ... <u>80</u>, ...
- The multiples of 8 are: 8, 16, 24, 32, <u>40</u>, 48, 56, 64, 72, <u>80</u>, ...

Among these multiples we find the common multiples 40 and 80. Of course, there are others as well, such as 120, 160, and so on. But 40 is the least (smallest) common multiple of 5 and 8.

It also so happens that 40 is $5 \cdot 8$. Indeed, $a \cdot b$ is *always* a common multiple of both a and b, but it is not always the *least* common multiple.

Example 3. Find the least common multiple of 4 and 6.

- The multiples of 4 are: 4, 8, <u>12</u>, 16, 20, <u>24</u>, 28, 32, <u>36</u>, 40, ...
- The multiples of 6 are: 6, <u>12</u>, 18, <u>24</u>, 30, <u>36</u>, 42, 48, 54, 60, ...

Among these multiples we find the common multiples 12, 24, and 36. Other common multiples would be 48, 60, 72, and so on. The *least* common multiple (LCM) is 12.

Note that the LCM of 4 and 6 is *not* $4 \cdot 6$.

1. Find the LCM of these numbers.

a. 2 and 6	**b.** 6 and 9
c. 14 and 8	**d.** 3 and 8
e. 7 and 10	**f.** 10 and 15

2. **a.** List four multiples of 6 that are less than 100.

   b. List four multiples of 250 that are greater than 1,200.

   c. What is the biggest multiple of 4 that is less than 100?

   d. What is the smallest multiple of 100 that is more than 1,000?

3. **a.** Find four numbers that are multiples of both 10 and 3.
   What is the LCM of 10 and 3?

   b. Find four numbers that are multiples of both 6 and 9.
   What is the LCM of 6 and 9?

   c. Find four numbers that are multiples of both 8 and 12.
   What is the LCM of 8 and 12?

4. Go back to exercise #1. Is the LCM of the two numbers also their product?

a. Is the LCM of 2 and 6 equal to 2 · 6?	**b.** Is the LCM of 6 and 9 equal to 6 · 9?
c. Is the LCM of 14 and 8 equal to 14 · 8?	**d.** Is the LCM of 3 and 8 equal to 3 · 8?
e. Is the LCM of 7 and 10 equal to 7 · 10?	**f.** Is the LCM of 10 and 15 equal to 10 · 15?

You may be wondering why sometimes the LCM is the product of the two numbers, and other times it is not. The key is:	If the numbers do not have any *common factors* (except 1), then their LCM is the product of the numbers.

5. Find the LCM of these numbers.

a. 3 and 4	**b.** 9 and 7
c. 10 and 5	**d.** 4 and 7
e. 2 and 10	**f.** 4 and 10

Remember? Before adding or subtracting *unlike* fractions, we need to convert them into equivalent fractions that have a **common denominator**.

Example 4 (on the right). The denominators 8 and 10 need to "go into" the common denominator. In other words, the common denominator must be **a multiple of both** 8 and 10. Naturally, the least common multiple is what we are looking for! The LCM of 8 and 10 is 40.

You *could* use any common multiple as the common denominator, (such as 80), but the LCM is the least (smallest) common denominator.

$$\frac{5}{8} + \frac{1}{10}$$
$$\downarrow \qquad \downarrow$$
$$\frac{25}{40} + \frac{4}{40} = \frac{29}{40}$$

6. Add or subtract the fractions. Give your answer in lowest terms.

a. $\dfrac{1}{9} + \dfrac{1}{8}$	**b.** $\dfrac{1}{12} + \dfrac{7}{8}$
c. $\dfrac{3}{7} - \dfrac{3}{10}$	**d.** $\dfrac{8}{9} - \dfrac{1}{6}$

7. Fill in the missing words:

The _____ common _____ is used in simplifying fractions, since we need to find a number that can divide ("go") into both the numerator and the denominator.

The _____ common _____ is used in adding unlike fractions, since we need to find a number that both denominators can divide ("go") into.

8. **a.** Draw a line from each number to the correct box.

    b. Which number is a "black sheep" (neither a factor nor a multiple of 24)?

    c. Which number is BOTH a factor and a multiple of 24?

240 8 48 4 96 24 1 2

a factor of 24	a multiple of 24

120 3 30 72 144 6 12

9. (*Challenge*) Can you find the LCM of *three* numbers?

a. 3 and 8 and 6	**b.** 2 and 6 and 10
c. 3 and 5 and 2	**d.** 4 and 7 and 8

(*This section is optional.*) There is a **quicker and more efficient way for finding the least common multiple of numbers**, where we do not have to make lists of multiples. It is based on prime factorization.

1. Write the prime factorization of the numbers.
2. The LCM is formed by taking ALL the factors from the numbers, without repeating any common factor.

Example 5. Find the LCM of 45 and 25.

1. The prime factorizations are $45 = 3 \cdot 3 \cdot 5$ and $25 = 5 \cdot 5$.

2. Form a number that is "all inclusive" or that includes all the factors from both numbers. It is $3 \cdot 3 \cdot 5 \cdot 5$, which equals 225.

Notice that $3 \cdot 3 \cdot 5 \cdot 5$ includes *both* $3 \cdot 3 \cdot 5$ and $5 \cdot 5$ but has no other factors beyond those.

Example 6. Find the LCM of 24 and 40.

1. The prime factorizations are $24 = 2 \cdot 2 \cdot 2 \cdot 3$ and $40 = 2 \cdot 2 \cdot 2 \cdot 5$.

2. The number that includes all the factors from both numbers is $2 \cdot 2 \cdot 2 \cdot 3 \cdot 5 = 120$.

10. Find the least common multiple of the numbers using any method.

a. 40 and 15	**b.** 20 and 24
c. 20 and 16	**d.** 50 and 120

11. Convert the fractions so they have the same denominator, and then compare them. Your work above can help!

a. $\dfrac{29}{40}$ and $\dfrac{11}{15}$	**b.** $\dfrac{11}{20}$ and $\dfrac{13}{24}$	**c.** $\dfrac{7}{20}$ and $\dfrac{5}{16}$	**d.** $\dfrac{39}{50}$ and $\dfrac{94}{120}$
↓ ↓	↓ ↓	↓ ↓	↓ ↓
☐	☐	☐	☐

Puzzle Corner   If the first day of the year is Tuesday, what day of the week is day number 236?

Mixed Review

1. Solve.

a. $10^4 \cdot 3$	**b.** 7^3	**c.** $10 \cdot 5^3$

2. Write in expanded form using exponents.

   a. 109,200

   b. 7,002,050

3. Andrew cut a 9-foot board into two pieces that are in a ratio of 3:5.
   Find the length of each of the two pieces.

4. Convert each division problem into another, equivalent division problem that you can solve in your head.

a. $\dfrac{16}{0.4} = \underline{\quad} =$	**b.** $\dfrac{7}{0.007} = \underline{\quad} =$	**c.** $\dfrac{99}{0.11} = \underline{\quad} =$

5. Multiply.

a. $100 \times 0.2 = \underline{\quad}$	**b.** $3 \times 1.02 = \underline{\quad}$	**c.** $0.9 \times 0.2 \times 0.5 = \underline{\quad}$
$120 \times 0.02 = \underline{\quad}$	$5 \times 3.02 = \underline{\quad}$	$30 \times 0.005 \times 0.2 = \underline{\quad}$

6. **a.** Draw a bar model to represent this situation:
      The ratio of girls to boys in a vocational school is 7:4.

   b. What is the ratio of boys to all students?

   c. If there are 748 students in all, how many are girls?
      How many are boys?

7. Liz is 150 cm tall, and her dad is 1.8 m tall. What percentage is Liz's height of her dad's height?

8. The Madison family spent $540 for groceries in one month. That was 24% of their total budget. How much was their total budget for the month?

9. Which is cheaper, a $180 camera discounted by 20%, or a $155 camera discounted by 10%?

10. Multiply using the distributive property.

a. $2(7m + 4) =$	**b.** $10(x + 6 + 2y) =$

11. Write an expression.

a. the quantity $5s$ plus 8, divided by 7

b. the quantity n plus 11, cubed

c. y more than 8

d. x divided by y squared

12. Solve the inequality $x - 3 < 0$ in the set $\{-2, -1, 0, 1, 2, 3\}$.

13. Divide, giving your answer as a decimal. If necessary, round the answers to three decimal digits.

a. $0.928 \div 0.3$	**b.** $\dfrac{7}{34}$

Chapter 6 Review

1. Factor the following composite numbers into their prime factors.

a. 81 /\	b. 26 /\	c. 65 /\
d. 96 /\	e. 124 /\	f. 450 /\

2. Simplify.

a. $\dfrac{28}{84} = \dfrac{4 \times 7}{21 \times 4} =$	b. $\dfrac{75}{160} =$
c. $\dfrac{222}{36} =$	d. $\dfrac{48}{120} =$

3. Find the least common multiple of these pairs of numbers.

a. 3 and 7	b. 10 and 8
c. 11 and 6	d. 6 and 8

4. Find the greatest common factor of the given number pairs.

a. 24 and 64	**b.** 100 and 75
c. 80 and 96	**d.** 78 and 96

5. Fill in with the words "multiple(s)" or "factor(s)."

- 25, 50, 75, 100, 125, and 150 are _____ of 25.

- 1, 2, 5, 10, 25, and 50 are _____ of 50.

- Each number has an infinite number of _____.

- Each number has a greatest _____.

- If a number x divides into another number y, we say x is a _____ of y.

b. List five different multiples of 15 that are less than 200 but more than 60.

c. Find five numbers that are multiples of both 4 and 7.
What is the LCM of 4 and 7?

6. First, find the GCF of the numbers. Then factor the expressions using the GCF.

a. GCF of 12 and 21 is _____   12 + 21 = ____ · ____ + ____ · ____ = ____ (____ + ____)
b. GCF of 45 and 70 is _____   45 + 70 = ____ (____ + ____)

7. Draw two rectangles, side by side, to represent the sum 42 + 30.

Chapter 7: Fractions
Introduction

This chapter begins with a review of fraction arithmetic from fifth grade—specifically, addition, subtraction, simplification, and multiplication of fractions. Then it focuses on the new topic: division of fractions.

The introductory lesson on the division of fractions presents the concept of reciprocal numbers and ties the reciprocity relationship to the idea that division is the appropriate operation to solve questions of the form, "How many times does this number fit into that number?" For example, we can write a division from the question, "How many times does 1/3 fit into 1?" The answer is, obviously, 3 times. So we can write the division $1 \div (1/3) = 3$ and the multiplication $3 \times (1/3) = 1$. These two numbers, 3/1 and 1/3, are reciprocal numbers because their product is 1.

Students learn to solve questions like that through using visual models and writing division sentences that match them. The eventual goal is to arrive at the shortcut for fraction division—that each division can be changed into a multiplication by taking the reciprocal of the divisor, which is often called the "invert (flip)-and-multiply" rule.

However, that "rule" is just a shortcut. It is necessary to memorize it, but memorizing a shortcut doesn't help students make sense conceptually out of the division of fractions—they also need to study the concept of division and use visual models to better understand the process involved.

In two lessons that follow, students apply what they have learned to solve problems involving fractions or fractional parts. A lot of the problems in these lessons are review in the sense that they involve previously learned concepts and are similar to problems students have solved earlier, but many involve the division of fractions, thus incorporating the new concept presented in this chapter.

Consider mixing the lessons from this chapter (or from some other chapter) with the lessons from the geometry chapter (which is a fairly long chapter). For example, the student could study these topics and geometry on alternate days, or study a little from both each day. Such, somewhat spiral, usage of the curriculum can help prevent boredom, and also to help students retain the concepts better.

The Lessons in Chapter 7

Helpful Resources on the Internet

ADDITION AND SUBTRACTION

Fraction Videos 1: Addition and Subtraction
My own videos that cover equivalent fractions, addition and subtraction of fractions and of mixed numbers.
http://www.mathmammoth.com/videos/fractions_1.php

Add Fractions Quiz
Use a pencil and paper to help you solve these fraction calculations involving the four operations.
http://www.transum.org/software/SW/Starter_of_the_day/Students/Fractions.asp?Level=3

Adding and Subtracting Fractions with Uncommon Denominators Tool at Conceptua Fractions
A tool that links a visual model to the procedure for adding two unlike fractions. A free registration is required.
https://www.conceptuamath.com/app/tool/adding-fractions-with-uncommon-denominators
https://www.conceptuamath.com/app/tool/subtracting-fractions-with-uncommon-denominators

Add and Subtract Mixed Numbers
Practice adding and subtracting mixed numbers with different denominators. Regrouping is required.
https://khanacademy.org/math/cc-fifth-grade-math/cc-5th-fractions-topic/tcc-5th-add-sub-mix-num-w-unlike-den/e/adding-and-subtracting-mixed-numbers-with-unlike-denominators-2

Drop Zone
Practice making a sum of one using fractions in this interactive online activity.
https://www.brainpop.com/games/dropzone/

Add and Subtract Fractions Word Problems
Practice solving fraction addition and subtraction word problems. The fractions in these problems have unlike denominators.
https://khanacademy.org/math/in-sixth-grade-math/fractions-1/addition-subtraction-fractions/e/adding-and-subtracting-fractions-with-unlike-denominators-word-problems

Old Egyptian Fractions
Puzzles to solve: Add fractions like a true Old Egyptian Math Cat!
http://www.mathcats.com/explore/oldegyptianfractions.html

MULTIPLICATION AND DIVISION

Fraction Videos 2: Multiplication and Division
My own videos that cover multiplying and dividing fractions.
http://www.mathmammoth.com/videos/fractions_2.php

Multiply Fractions Jeopardy
A jeopardy-style game. Choose a question by clicking on the tile that shows the number of points you will win.
http://www.quia.com/cb/95583.html

Fraction of a Number
Practice finding fractional parts of various numbers in this interactive online exercise.
https://www.mathplayground.com/fractions_fractionof.html

Multiply Mixed Numbers Quiz
A self-check quiz requiring application of the four operations applied to mixed numbers.
http://www.transum.org/software/SW/Starter_of_the_day/Students/Mixed_Numbers.asp?Level=3

Multiply Fractions Word Problems
Solve and interpret fraction multiplication word problems in this interactive online exercise.
https://www.khanacademy.org/math/in-seventh-grade-math/fractions-decimals/multiplicaiton-fractions/e/multiplying-fractions-by-fractions-word-problems

Interactive Area Model for the Multiplication of Fractions
In this interactive activity, you will learn how to use area models to multiply fractions.
https://www.learner.org/courses/learningmath/number/session9/part_a/try.html

Multiplying Fractions with Cross-Canceling Worksheets
Create customized worksheets for multiplication of fractions with cross-canceling.
http://www.math-aids.com/Fractions/Multiplying_Fractions_Cross_Cancel.html

Math Basketball - Dividing Fractions Game
First make a basket, and then you get to solve a fraction division problem with multiple-choice answers.
http://www.math-play.com/math-basketball-dividing-fractions-game/math-basketball-dividing-fractions-game.html

Soccer Math - Dividing Fractions Game
In order to kick the ball and score points, you first have to answer math problems correctly.
http://www.math-play.com/soccer-math-dividing-fractions-game/soccer-math-dividing-fractions-game.html

Divide Fractions "Strict"
Enter the values into the calculator that are shown in the illustrations to divide the mixed numbers.
http://www.visualfractions.com/DivideStrict/

Divide Fractions Quiz
Solve the problems in this online quiz with the help of a pencil and paper.
http://www.transum.org/software/SW/Starter_of_the_day/Students/Fractions.asp?Level=8

Dividing Fractions Word Problems
Practice solving word problems by dividing fractions by fractions.
https://www.khanacademy.org/math/on-sixth-grade-math/on-number-sense-numeration/on-fractions/e/dividing-fractions-by-fractions-word-problems

Fraction Worksheets: Addition, Subtraction, Multiplication, and Division
Create custom-made worksheets for fraction addition, subtraction, multiplication, and division.
http://www.homeschoolmath.net/worksheets/fraction.php

WORD PROBLEMS

Thinking Blocks - Fractions
Model and solve fraction word problems. Choose the model titled "Remainders" to practice the concepts studied in the lesson Problem Solving with Fractions 1.
http://www.mathplayground.com/tb_fractions/index.html

Thinking Blocks - Fractions
Model and solve fraction word problems. Choose the model titled "Find the total" to practice the concepts studied in the lesson Problem Solving with Fractions 2.
http://www.mathplayground.com/tb_fractions/index.html

GENERAL

Fraction Games
These fun fractions games reinforce ordering, identifying, converting and drawing fractions, as well as equivalent fractions and fractions operations.
http://mrnussbaum.com/fraction-games/

Fraction Games at Sheppard Software
Games for practicing adding and subtracting fractions, simplifying fractions, and finding equivalent fractions and the fraction of a set.
http://www.sheppardsoftware.com/mathgames/menus/fractions.htm

Numerate Game for Fractions
The object of this two-player game is to form equations using the available tiles. Drag tiles onto the board to form an equation and click the "confirm" button.
http://www.transum.org/Maths/Game/Numerate/Default.asp?Level=3

Fraction Calculations Quiz
Practice fraction arithmetic with all four operations in this interactive online quiz.
http://www.transum.org/software/SW/Starter_of_the_day/Students/Fractions.asp?Level=9

Fraction Models
Explore improper fractions, mixed numbers, decimals, and percentages. The activity includes several models: bar, area, pie, and set. Adjust numerators and denominators to see how they alter the representations of the fractions and the models.
http://illuminations.nctm.org/Activity.aspx?id=3519

Fractional Hi Lo
The computer has selected a fraction. You make guesses and it tells you if your guess was too high or too low.
http://www.theproblemsite.com/games/hilo.asp

Fractions Workshop
Reinforce your fraction skills with this interactive activity. Choose which area you would like to practice and the number of problems.
http://mrnussbaum.com/fractions-workshop-2/

Conceptua Math Fractions Tools
Free and interactive tools for fractions: identify them, add or subtract them, estimate with them, compare them, find equivalent fractions, multiply or divide them, find common denominators, and more. Each activity uses several fraction models such as fraction circles, horizontal and vertical bars, number lines, *etc.* that allow students to develop a conceptual understanding of fractions. A free registration is required.
http://www.conceptuamath.com/app/tool-library

Fraction Lessons at MathExpression.com
Tutorials, examples, and videos to explain all of the basic topics in fractions.
http://www.mathexpression.com/learning-fractions.html

Visual Math Learning
Free tutorials with some interactivity about all the fraction operations. Emphasizes visual models and lets students interact with those.
http://www.visualmathlearning.com/pre_algebra/chapter_9/chap_9.html

Online Fraction Calculator
Add, subtract, multiply, or divide fractions and mixed numbers.
http://www.homeschoolmath.net/worksheets/fraction_calculator.php

Fraction Worksheets: Addition, Subtraction, Multiplication, and Division
Create custom-made worksheets for the four operations with fractions and mixed numbers.
http://www.homeschoolmath.net/worksheets/fraction.php

Fraction Worksheets: Equivalent Fractions, Simplifying, Convert to Mixed Numbers
Create custom-made worksheets for some other fraction operations.
http://www.homeschoolmath.net/worksheets/fraction-b.php

Review: Add and Subtract Fractions and Mixed Numbers

Example 1. Add $\dfrac{5}{6} + 2\dfrac{5}{8}$.

We need to convert unlike fractions into equivalent fractions that have a common denominator before we can add them. The common denominator must be a **multiple of both 6 and 8** (a *common* multiple).

Naturally, $6 \times 8 = 48$ is one common multiple of 6 and 8. We could use 48. However, it is better to use 24, which is the *least* common multiple (LCM) of 6 and 8, because it leads to easier calculations.

The common denominator is 24:

$$\dfrac{5}{6} + 2\dfrac{5}{8}$$

$$\downarrow \qquad \downarrow$$

$$\dfrac{20}{24} + 2\dfrac{15}{24} = 2\dfrac{35}{24} = 3\dfrac{11}{24}$$

1. Write the missing addition sentences.

a.	b. Common denominator 36	c. Common denominator 20
(figures) $\dfrac{\;\;}{\;\;} + \dfrac{\;\;}{\;\;}$ ... $= \dfrac{\;\;}{\;\;} + \dfrac{\;\;}{\;\;} = \dfrac{\;\;}{\;\;}$	$\dfrac{3}{4} + \dfrac{1}{9}$ $\;\;\downarrow\;\;\;\;\downarrow$ $\dfrac{\;\;}{\;\;} + \dfrac{\;\;}{\;\;} = \dfrac{\;\;}{\;\;}$	$\dfrac{7}{10} + \dfrac{1}{4}$ $\;\;\downarrow\;\;\;\;\downarrow$ $\dfrac{\;\;}{\;\;} + \dfrac{\;\;}{\;\;} = \dfrac{\;\;}{\;\;}$

2. Find a common denominator (c.d.) that will work for adding or subtracting these fractions. Remember that the *best* possible choice for the common denominator (but not the only one) is the LCM of the denominators.

Fractions	c.d.		Fractions	c.d.		Fractions	c.d.
a. $\dfrac{5}{16}$ and $\dfrac{1}{6}$		**b.** $\dfrac{1}{12}$ and $\dfrac{4}{9}$		**c.** $\dfrac{5}{6}$ and $\dfrac{3}{8}$	
d. $\dfrac{1}{12}$ and $\dfrac{2}{5}$		**e.** $\dfrac{11}{15}$ and $\dfrac{13}{20}$		**f.** $\dfrac{45}{100}$ and $\dfrac{9}{20}$	

3. Add and subtract. Use the common denominator you found in the previous exercise.

a. $\dfrac{5}{16} + \dfrac{1}{6}$	**b.** $3\dfrac{1}{12} + 1\dfrac{4}{9}$	**c.** $\dfrac{5}{6} - \dfrac{3}{8}$
d. $2\dfrac{5}{12} + \dfrac{4}{5}$	**e.** $5\dfrac{11}{15} - 2\dfrac{3}{20}$	**f.** $\dfrac{45}{100} + \dfrac{9}{20}$

Regroup in subtraction, if necessary.	We can use the same idea (regrouping) when the fractions are written horizontally.

$$9\frac{14}{13}$$
$$10\frac{1}{13}$$
$$-\ 5\frac{5}{13}$$
$$\overline{\qquad}$$
$$4\frac{9}{13}$$

Example 2. Here we regroup **one** as 13/13. This leaves 9 wholes. There is already 1/13 in the column of the fractional parts, so in total we get 14/13.

Example 3. Take one of the 7 wholes, think of it as 9/9, and regroup that with the fractional parts (with 2/9). Instead of 7 wholes, we are left with 6, and instead of 2/9, we get 11/9.

$$7\frac{2}{9}-3\frac{8}{9}$$
$$\downarrow \qquad \downarrow$$
$$6\frac{11}{9}-3\frac{8}{9}=3\frac{3}{9}$$

4. Subtract.

a.
$$7\frac{3}{9}$$
$$-\ 2\frac{7}{9}$$
$$\overline{\qquad}$$

b.
$$18\frac{1}{10}$$
$$-\ 5\frac{9}{10}$$
$$\overline{\qquad}$$

c.
$$10\frac{1}{15}$$
$$-\ 3\frac{8}{15}$$
$$\overline{\qquad}$$

d. $16\frac{3}{9}-9\frac{8}{9}$

e. $7\frac{3}{14}-2\frac{10}{14}$

5. Subtract. First write equivalent fractions with the same denominator.

a. $\quad 3\frac{3}{4}\ \rightarrow\ 3\frac{\ }{\ }$
$\quad -\ 1\frac{1}{6}\ \rightarrow\ -\ 1\frac{\ }{\ }$
$\overline{\qquad}$

b. $\quad 3\frac{3}{8}\ \rightarrow$
$\quad -\ 1\frac{5}{12}\ \rightarrow\ -$
$\overline{\qquad}$

c. $\quad 8\frac{9}{11}\ \rightarrow$
$\quad -\ 5\frac{1}{2}\ \rightarrow\ -$
$\overline{\qquad}$

6. Figure out and explain how these subtractions were done!

Emma's way: $9\frac{2}{17}-3\frac{8}{17}$

$$=(9-3)+\left(\frac{2}{17}-\frac{8}{17}\right)=6-\frac{6}{17}=5\frac{11}{17}$$

Joe's method: $5\frac{3}{14}-2\frac{9}{14}$
$$\downarrow$$
$$5\frac{3}{14}-2\frac{3}{14}-\frac{6}{14}$$
$$=\ 3\ -\frac{6}{14}=2\frac{8}{14}$$

35

7. Sarah used 2 1/4 C of whole wheat flour, 3/4 C of rye flour, 1 3/8 C of white flour, 3/4 C of oat flour, and 5/8 C of corn flour for a multi-grain bread. Find the total volume of flour she used in the bread.

8. Joe has a piece of wood that is 9 inches long. If he cuts off two pieces that are each 1 5/8 in long, then how long will the remaining piece be?

When adding or subtracting *three* fractions, **find a common denominator for all of them.** You can always use the product of the denominators as your common denominator. So, we *could* use $6 \times 7 \times 2 = 84$ as a common denominator.

However, it *may be* more efficient to use the LCM of the denominators if it is smaller. In this case, the LCM of 6, 7, and 2 is 42, so it is better (leads to easier calculations) than using 84.

Another option would be to add the first two fractions (5/6 and 5/7) to get 65/42, and then to subtract the third fraction, 1/2, from that result.

Example 4.

$$\frac{5}{6} + \frac{5}{7} - \frac{1}{2}$$
$$\downarrow \qquad \downarrow \qquad \downarrow$$
$$\frac{35}{42} + \frac{30}{42} - \frac{21}{42} = \frac{44}{42} = 1\frac{1}{21}$$

---

9. Add or subtract the fractions.

a. $\dfrac{5}{12} + \dfrac{1}{6} + \dfrac{1}{3}$	**b.** $\dfrac{2}{7} + \dfrac{1}{2} - \dfrac{1}{4}$
c. $\dfrac{1}{10} + \dfrac{2}{5} + \dfrac{1}{3}$	**d.** $\dfrac{19}{20} - \dfrac{1}{3} - \dfrac{1}{4}$
e. $\dfrac{7}{8} - \dfrac{1}{5} + \dfrac{2}{3}$	**f.** $\dfrac{7}{6} - \dfrac{3}{5} + \dfrac{3}{4}$

10. Compare the fractions. Write <, = , or > between each pair. If you need to, change the fractions to equivalent fractions with the same denominator. However, if you can, compare the fractions without doing that.

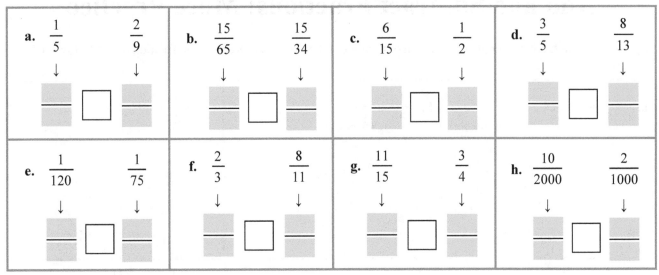

| a. $\dfrac{1}{5}$ | $\dfrac{2}{9}$ | b. $\dfrac{15}{65}$ | $\dfrac{15}{34}$ | c. $\dfrac{6}{15}$ | $\dfrac{1}{2}$ | d. $\dfrac{3}{5}$ | $\dfrac{8}{13}$ |

| e. $\dfrac{1}{120}$ | $\dfrac{1}{75}$ | f. $\dfrac{2}{3}$ | $\dfrac{8}{11}$ | g. $\dfrac{11}{15}$ | $\dfrac{3}{4}$ | h. $\dfrac{10}{2000}$ | $\dfrac{2}{1000}$ |

11. Find the value of the expressions.

a. Find the value of $x - y - 1$ when	**b.** Find the value of $5 - x - y$ when
$x = 8\dfrac{1}{9}$ and $y = 2\dfrac{5}{9}$	$x = 2\dfrac{1}{8}$ and $y = \dfrac{11}{12}$

12. (Optional.) Solve the equations. Hint: If the fractions confuse you, *first* change the equation into an easier one that uses whole numbers. Think how the equation would be solved if it had whole numbers. Then solve the original equation the same way.

a. $x + \dfrac{1}{2} = 7\dfrac{1}{3}$	**b.** $x - 5\dfrac{7}{10} = 4\dfrac{3}{5}$
c. $8\dfrac{4}{7} + x = 10\dfrac{2}{5}$	**d.** $5\dfrac{1}{9} - x = 2\dfrac{1}{3}$

Add and Subtract Fractions: More Practice

1. Add or subtract. Give your answer as a mixed number when possible. Reduce the fractional part to lowest terms.

a. $\dfrac{17}{18} + \dfrac{2}{9}$	**b.** $\dfrac{11}{30} + \dfrac{7}{12}$	**c.** $\dfrac{13}{22} + \dfrac{3}{4}$
d. $6\dfrac{7}{10} - 1\dfrac{3}{20}$	**e.** $4\dfrac{7}{8} - 1\dfrac{1}{3}$	**f.** $15\dfrac{9}{10} - 3\dfrac{31}{100}$

2. Subtract. First write equivalent fractions with the same denominator.

a. $\quad 5\dfrac{1}{2} \quad \rightarrow \quad 5\dfrac{}{}$ $-\ 1\dfrac{7}{12} \quad \rightarrow \quad -\ 1\dfrac{}{}$	**b.** $\quad 12\dfrac{1}{9}$ $-\ 5\dfrac{2}{3}$	**c.** $\quad 33\dfrac{1}{3}$ $-\ 17\dfrac{6}{7}$
d. $\quad 8\dfrac{1}{9}$ $-\ 2\dfrac{7}{12}$	**e.** $\quad 86\dfrac{6}{7}$ $-\ 45\dfrac{1}{8}$	**f.** $\quad 53\dfrac{1}{6}$ $-\ 40\dfrac{6}{7}$

3. Add or subtract these fractions to solve the riddle! Give your answer as a mixed number, if possible, and put the fractional part into lowest terms.

I. $2\dfrac{7}{15} + 1\dfrac{1}{3}$

P. $\dfrac{4}{7} - \dfrac{1}{5}$

V. $6\dfrac{1}{15} + 5\dfrac{1}{2}$

I. $9\dfrac{7}{20} - 3\dfrac{2}{10}$

U. $2\dfrac{1}{8} - \dfrac{1}{6}$

T. $9\dfrac{1}{12} - 2\dfrac{9}{30}$

D. $3\dfrac{7}{12} - 2\dfrac{1}{3}$

G. $9\dfrac{1}{10} - 4\dfrac{3}{4}$

E. $5\dfrac{5}{14} - 3\dfrac{1}{4}$

D. $\dfrac{5}{22} + 2\dfrac{1}{11}$

L. $4\dfrac{5}{9} - 1\dfrac{1}{12}$

M. $2\dfrac{1}{4} - \dfrac{1}{3}$

I. $2\dfrac{4}{5} + \dfrac{11}{24}$

I. $3\dfrac{2}{7} - 2\dfrac{1}{5}$

I. $5\dfrac{2}{9} - \dfrac{11}{27}$

D. $6\dfrac{3}{20} - 3\dfrac{1}{12}$

N. $\dfrac{3}{8} - \dfrac{1}{12}$

L. $4\dfrac{7}{8} - 1\dfrac{1}{12}$

Why did the amoeba flunk the math test? Because it...

$1\frac{11}{12}$	$1\frac{23}{24}$	$3\frac{17}{36}$	$6\frac{47}{60}$	$3\frac{4}{5}$	$\frac{13}{35}$	$3\frac{19}{24}$	$3\frac{31}{120}$	$2\frac{3}{28}$	$1\frac{1}{4}$

by

$2\frac{7}{22}$	$6\frac{3}{20}$	$11\frac{17}{30}$	$1\frac{3}{35}$	$3\frac{1}{15}$	$4\frac{22}{27}$	$\frac{7}{24}$	$4\frac{7}{20}$

39

4. Solve the expressions. Give each answer in the lowest terms and find it in the grid. With a bright color, color in the squares of the grid that contain the answers. Color the other squares with a dark color. Note the pattern.

a. $3\dfrac{1}{3} - 1\dfrac{2}{15} + 1\dfrac{2}{5}$

$5\dfrac{1}{48}$	$2\dfrac{7}{24}$	$2\dfrac{5}{48}$	$5\dfrac{3}{50}$	$1\dfrac{1}{60}$
$3\dfrac{11}{48}$	$6\dfrac{1}{8}$	$4\dfrac{5}{24}$	$3\dfrac{17}{24}$	$2\dfrac{1}{50}$
$3\dfrac{53}{66}$	$2\dfrac{19}{48}$	$2\dfrac{9}{50}$	$4\dfrac{1}{8}$	$3\dfrac{7}{8}$
$3\dfrac{1}{5}$	$3\dfrac{13}{15}$	$3\dfrac{3}{5}$	$5\dfrac{13}{66}$	$5\dfrac{4}{5}$
$4\dfrac{53}{66}$	$1\dfrac{29}{60}$	$4\dfrac{11}{50}$	$7\dfrac{39}{50}$	$6\dfrac{41}{50}$

b. $\dfrac{7}{10} + \dfrac{2}{25} + 1\dfrac{2}{5}$

c. $6\dfrac{67}{100} - 1\dfrac{2}{5} + 1\dfrac{11}{20}$

d. $3\dfrac{1}{2} - \dfrac{2}{3} - \dfrac{7}{16}$

g. $3\dfrac{7}{20} - 1\dfrac{1}{12} - 1\dfrac{1}{4}$

e. $\dfrac{13}{16} + 2\dfrac{1}{12} + 2\dfrac{3}{24}$

h. $5\dfrac{1}{6} + 1\dfrac{3}{8} - 2\dfrac{1}{3}$

f. $7\dfrac{7}{8} - 1\dfrac{1}{2} - 2\dfrac{1}{4}$

i. $19\dfrac{7}{11} - 10\dfrac{1}{3} - 4\dfrac{1}{2}$

Review: Multiplying Fractions 1

<table>
<tr>
<td>
The shortcut for multiplying fractions is:
<ul>
<li>Multiply the numerators.</li>
<li>Multiply the denominators.</li>
</ul>
</td>
<td>

$$\frac{6}{7} \times \frac{5}{2} \times \frac{1}{3} = \frac{6 \times 5 \times 1}{7 \times 2 \times 3} = \frac{30}{42} = \frac{5}{7}$$

</td>
</tr>
<tr>
<td>
To multiply mixed numbers, first write them <u>as fractions</u>, then multiply.

$$2\frac{1}{3} \times 1\frac{1}{10} = \frac{7}{3} \times \frac{11}{10} = \frac{7 \times 11}{3 \times 10} = \frac{77}{30} = 2\frac{17}{30}$$
</td>
<td>
If one of the factors is a whole number, it multiplies the numerator only.

$$6 \times \frac{11}{12} = \frac{6 \times 11}{12} = \frac{66}{12} = \frac{11}{2} = 5\frac{1}{2}$$
</td>
</tr>
</table>

1. Multiply. Give your answers as mixed numbers. Put the fractional part into lowest terms.

a. $5 \times \dfrac{7}{8}$	**b.** $\dfrac{2}{7} \times \dfrac{5}{6}$
c. $\dfrac{9}{10} \times \dfrac{6}{7} \times \dfrac{1}{2}$	**d.** $1\dfrac{1}{3} \times 2\dfrac{2}{3}$
e. $\dfrac{1}{10} \times 3\dfrac{1}{5}$	**f.** $2\dfrac{5}{6} \times 10 \times \dfrac{1}{2}$

2. Find the volume of a cube with 1 1/4-inch sides.

3. Mary sewed cloth squares together to make a quilt. The finished quilt measured
   9 squares by 20 squares, and each square had sides 5 1/2 inches long.

   a. What is the area of each of the individual squares?

   b. What is the total area of Mary's quilt in square inches?

You have already learned to use **factoring** when simplifying.
The example on the right shows simplifying 96/144.

$$\frac{96}{144} = \frac{\overset{2}{\cancel{8}} \times \overset{1}{\cancel{12}}}{\underset{3}{\cancel{12}} \times \underset{1}{\cancel{12}}} = \frac{2}{3}$$

You have also learned how to simplify **"criss-cross."** To simplify 45/150, we cancel the 5s from the numerator and the denominator. Then we simplify 9 and 30 into 3 and 10.

$$\frac{45}{150} = \frac{\overset{1}{\cancel{5}} \times \overset{3}{\cancel{9}}}{\underset{10}{\cancel{30}} \times \underset{1}{\cancel{5}}} = \frac{3}{10}$$

In a similar manner, you can simplify fractions *before* multiplying.

Compare the two examples on the right. They show the same problem.

The first one (above right) is written out with an extra step, whereas the one below is written without the extra step.
In both cases, the simplifying is done *before* multiplying.

$$\frac{7}{6} \times \frac{3}{9} = \frac{7 \times \overset{1}{\cancel{3}}}{\underset{2}{\cancel{6}} \times 9} = \frac{7}{18}$$

$$\frac{7}{\underset{2}{\cancel{6}}} \times \frac{\overset{1}{\cancel{3}}}{9} = \frac{7}{18}$$

4. Simplify before multiplying, and solve the riddle.

E. $\dfrac{3}{10} \times \dfrac{1}{3} =$

O. $\dfrac{2}{6} \times \dfrac{5}{7} =$

M. $\dfrac{4}{10} \times \dfrac{1}{3} =$

I. $7 \times \dfrac{5}{21} =$

W. $\dfrac{4}{5} \times \dfrac{3}{6} =$

S. $\dfrac{7}{40} \times 15 =$

A. $\dfrac{5}{6} \times \dfrac{2}{4} =$

L. $\dfrac{2}{9} \times \dfrac{9}{11} =$

E. $\dfrac{3}{10} \times \dfrac{3}{9} =$

N. $\dfrac{16}{24} \times 8 =$

P. $\dfrac{4}{8} \times \dfrac{1}{3} =$

R. $\dfrac{2}{6} \times \dfrac{3}{9} =$

$\frac{5}{12}$	$\frac{1}{9}$	$\frac{1}{10}$	$\frac{21}{8}$	$\frac{5}{3}$	$\frac{2}{15}$	$\frac{1}{6}$	$\frac{2}{11}$	$\frac{1}{10}$	$\frac{16}{3}$	$\frac{5}{21}$	$\frac{2}{5}$

These problems !

42

Use multiplication to find a fractional part of a fraction. The word "of" translates into multiplication.	
How much is $\frac{3}{4}$ of ? Since "of" becomes ×, we get the multiplication $\frac{3}{4} \times \frac{8}{12} = \frac{\overset{1}{\cancel{3}}}{\underset{1}{\cancel{4}}} \times \frac{\overset{2}{\cancel{8}}}{\underset{4}{\cancel{12}}} = \frac{2}{4} = \frac{1}{2}.$	But, how can we make sense of that answer 1/2? If you have 8 slices of a pie that was originally cut into twelfths, and you take 3/4 *of* those 8 slices, you will end up with 6 slices (of the original 12). And 6/12 is 1/2. $\frac{3}{4}$ of is .

5. The pictures show how much pizza is left. Find the given part of it. Write a multiplication sentence.

a. Find $\frac{1}{2}$ of 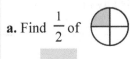 $\frac{1}{2} \times \dfrac{\ }{\ } =$	**b.** Find $\frac{2}{3}$ of 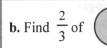 $\dfrac{\ }{\ } \times \dfrac{\ }{\ } =$	**c.** Find $\frac{1}{4}$ of × =
d. Find $\frac{9}{10}$ of × =	**e.** Find $\frac{1}{6}$ of × =	**f.** Find $\frac{3}{8}$ of × =

6. Rewrite the ingredients for the pancake recipe as 3/4 of the original amounts.

Pancakes	Pancakes
1 3/4 c milk	_____ milk
2 eggs	_____ eggs
2 c flour	_____ c flour
2 1/2 tsp baking powder	_____ tsp baking powder
1/2 tsp salt	_____ tsp salt
1 tsp cinnamon	_____ tsp cinnamon

7. Isabella was riding her bicycle from her house to her friend's, which was 3/4 mile away. Then, 2/3 of the way there, she realized that she had forgotten something, so she had to return home. What distance did Isabella ride her bicycle from her home to the point where she turned back and then home again? Calculate the distance in two ways:

a. Using fractions.

b. Using decimals.

Review: Multiplying Fractions 2

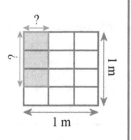

Fraction multiplication and area

Study the picture. The colored rectangle is a fraction of the one-meter square. Its top measures 1/3 m, and its side measures 3/4 m. To find its area, we multiply those fractions: $\dfrac{1}{3}$ m $\times \dfrac{3}{4}$ m $= \dfrac{3}{12}$ m^2 $= \dfrac{1}{4}$ m^2.

The whole square is 1 m^2. So the colored rectangle is 3/12 = 1/4 of that area, or 1/4 m^2.

1. Write the multiplication for the area of the colored rectangle. In (c) and (d), do not include any units in the multiplication (simply write the fractions without any units).

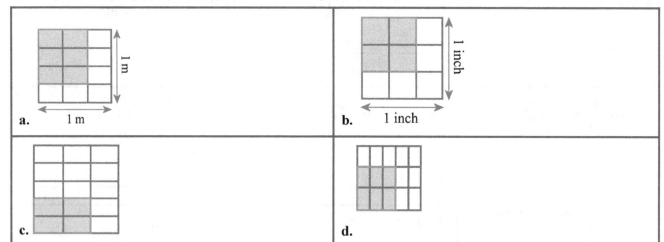

2. Multiply. Shade a rectangle in the grid to illustrate the multiplications.

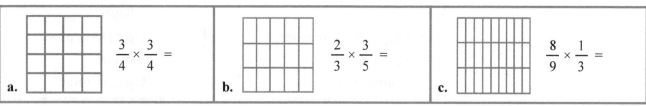

3. These situations use mixed numbers. Be careful!

a. Write a multiplication.

b. Shade a rectangle to illustrate the multiplication.

$$1\frac{1}{4} \times 1\frac{3}{4} =$$

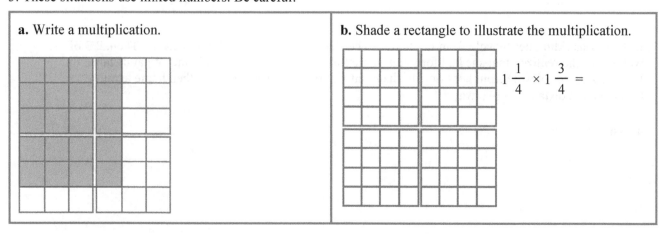

44

4. What is the area of a town that extends over a 4 1/4 km by 3 3/8 km rectangle?

5. **a.** Find the area of the *white* rectangle inside of the larger rectangle.

   b. Find the area of the shaded part.

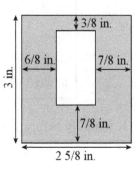

6. Find the price for 2 3/4 pounds of nuts if one pound costs $8.

7. Find the price for 5/8 of a pound of nuts if one pound costs $10.

8. Let's change the above problem so that the price is the *decimal* number $10.38.
How much would 1 3/8 pounds of nuts cost?
Hint: Change the mixed number to a decimal.

9. Make equivalent fractions by multiplying the given fraction by different forms of the number 1.

a. Multiply the fraction by $\frac{5}{5}$.	**b.** Multiply the fraction by $\frac{3}{3}$.	**c.** Multiply the fraction by $\frac{9}{9}$.
 $\times \dfrac{2}{3} =$	 $\times \dfrac{7}{10} =$	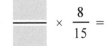 $\times \dfrac{8}{15} =$

10. Is the result of multiplication more, less, or equal to the original number? Write $<$, $>$, or $=$. You do not have to calculate anything.

a. $\frac{11}{12} \times 21$ ☐ 21	**b.** $2\frac{1}{3} \times 19$ ☐ 19	**c.** $\frac{16}{16} \times 105$ ☐ 105

You can simplify several times before multiplying.			
$\dfrac{\overset{1}{\cancel{3}}}{15} \times \dfrac{5}{\underset{2}{\cancel{6}}}$	$\dfrac{\overset{1}{\cancel{3}}}{\underset{3}{\cancel{15}}} \times \dfrac{\overset{1}{\cancel{5}}}{\underset{2}{\cancel{6}}} = \dfrac{1}{6}$	$\dfrac{\overset{1}{\cancel{3}}}{\underset{5}{\cancel{15}}} \times \dfrac{7}{14}$	$\dfrac{\overset{1}{\cancel{3}}}{\underset{5}{\cancel{15}}} \times \dfrac{\overset{1}{\cancel{7}}}{\underset{2}{\cancel{14}}} = \dfrac{1}{10}$
First simplify 3 and 6 into 1 and 2.	Then simplify 5 and 15 into 1 and 3.	First simplify 3 and 15 into 1 and 5.	Then simplify 7 and 14 into 1 and 2.

11. Simplify before you multiply.

a. $\dfrac{8}{12} \times \dfrac{6}{12}$	**b.** $\dfrac{3}{10} \times \dfrac{2}{18}$	**c.** $\dfrac{2}{30} \times \dfrac{10}{11}$
d. $\dfrac{7}{21} \times \dfrac{3}{4}$	**e.** $\dfrac{2}{16} \times \dfrac{8}{9}$	**f.** $\dfrac{18}{24} \times \dfrac{8}{9}$

12. Try your simplifying skills with multiplying three fractions.

a. $\dfrac{5}{4} \times \dfrac{12}{9} \times \dfrac{3}{15}$	**b.** $\dfrac{8}{10} \times \dfrac{15}{27} \times \dfrac{9}{16}$
c. $\dfrac{1}{18} \times \dfrac{24}{33} \times \dfrac{9}{20}$	**d.** $\dfrac{3}{5} \times \dfrac{15}{18} \times \dfrac{16}{50}$

a. Simplify: $\dfrac{60}{48} \times \dfrac{36}{90} =$ Puzzle Corner	**b.** Draw a rectangle to illustrate $3\dfrac{1}{3} \times 1\dfrac{2}{3}$. 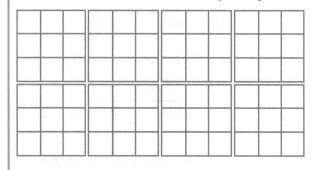 **c.** Use your drawing to show a fellow student that you *cannot* multiply this way: 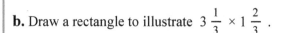 $3\dfrac{1}{3} \times 1\dfrac{2}{3}$ is simply 3×1 and $(1/3) \times (2/3)$, or 3 2/9.

Dividing Fractions: Reciprocal Numbers

First, let's review a little.

How many times does one number go into another?

From this situation, you can always write a division, even if the numbers are fractions!

How many times does go into ?

Three times. We write the division: $2 \div \dfrac{2}{3} = 3$.

Then check the division: $3 \times \dfrac{2}{3} = \dfrac{6}{3} = 2$.

1. Solve. Write a division. Then write a multiplication that checks your division.

a. How many times does ⬭ go into ⬤⬤⬤ ?

$3 \div \dfrac{1}{3} =$ _____

Check: _____ $\times \dfrac{1}{3} =$

b. How many times does ◻ go into ⊕⊕ ?

 ÷ _____ = _____

Check: _____ × _____ =

c. How many times does ◁ go into 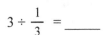 ?

÷ _____ = _____

Check:

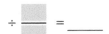

d. How many times does ⊕ go into ⬤⬤⬤⊕ ?

÷ _____ = _____

Check:

2. Solve. Think how many times the fraction goes into the whole number. Can you find a *pattern* or a *shortcut*?

a. $3 \div \dfrac{1}{6} =$	**b.** $4 \div \dfrac{1}{5} =$	**c.** $3 \div \dfrac{1}{10} =$	**d.** $5 \div \dfrac{1}{10} =$
e. $7 \div \dfrac{1}{4} =$	**f.** $4 \div \dfrac{1}{8} =$	**g.** $4 \div \dfrac{1}{10} =$	**h.** $9 \div \dfrac{1}{8} =$

The shortcut is this:

$5 \div \dfrac{1}{4}$
↓ ↓
$5 \times 4 = 20$

$3 \div \dfrac{1}{8}$
↓ ↓
$3 \times 8 = 24$

$9 \div \dfrac{1}{7}$
↓ ↓
$9 \times 7 = 63$

That is, *multiply the number by the reciprocal of the divisor.* Notice that 1/4 inverted (upside down) is 4/1 or simply 4. We call 1/4 and 4 **reciprocal numbers,** or just **reciprocals.** So the shortcut is: *multiply by the reciprocal of the divisor.*

Does the shortcut make sense to you? For example, consider the problem 5 ÷ (1/4). Since 1/4 goes into 1 exactly four times, it must go into 5 exactly 5 × 4 = 20 times.

> **Two numbers are reciprocal numbers (or reciprocals) of each other if, when multiplied, they make 1.**
>
> | | |
> |---|---|
> | $\frac{3}{4}$ is a reciprocal of $\frac{4}{3}$, because $\frac{3}{4} \times \frac{4}{3} = \frac{12}{12} = 1$. | $\frac{1}{7}$ is a reciprocal of 7, because $\frac{1}{7} \times 7 = \frac{7}{7} = 1$. |
>
> You can find the reciprocal of a fraction $\frac{m}{n}$ by inverting the numerator and denominator: $\frac{n}{m}$.
>
> This works, because $\frac{m}{n} \times \frac{n}{m} = \frac{n \times m}{m \times n} = 1$.
>
> To find the reciprocal of a <u>mixed number</u>, first write it as a fraction, then invert it.
>
> Since $2\frac{3}{4} = \frac{11}{4}$, its reciprocal number is $\frac{4}{11}$.

3. Find the reciprocal numbers. Then write a multiplication with the given number and its reciprocal.

a. $\frac{5}{8}$	**b.** $\frac{1}{9}$	**c.** $1\frac{7}{8}$	**d.** 32	**e.** $2\frac{1}{8}$
$\frac{5}{8} \times \frac{}{} = 1$	$\frac{}{} \times \frac{}{} = 1$	$\frac{}{} \times \frac{}{} = 1$	$32 \times \frac{}{} = 1$	$\frac{}{} \times \frac{}{} = 1$

4. Write a division sentence to match each multiplication above.

a. $1 \div \frac{}{} = \frac{}{}$	**b.** $1 \div \frac{}{} = \frac{}{}$	**c.** $1 \div \frac{}{} = \frac{}{}$	**d.** $\underline{} \div \frac{}{} = \frac{}{}$	**e.** $\underline{} \div \frac{}{} = \frac{}{}$

Read the following explanation and really try to understand it. It is important!

> **Now let's try to make some sense visually out of how reciprocal numbers fit into the division of fractions.**
>
> We can think of the division problem **1 ÷ (2/5)** as asking, **"How many times does 2/5 fit into 1?"**
>
> Using pictures: How many times does go into ?
>
> ---
>
> From the picture we can see that goes into two times, and then we have 1/5 left over.
>
> But how many times does $\frac{2}{5}$ fit into the leftover piece, $\frac{1}{5}$? How many times does go into △ ?
>
> ---
>
> That is like trying to fit a TWO-part piece into a hole that holds just ONE part.
> **Only 1/2 of the two-part piece fits!** And 2/5 fits into 1/5 exactly half a time.
>
> ---
>
> So we found that, in total, 2/5 fits into one exactly **2 1/2 times**. We can write the division $1 \div \frac{2}{5} = 2\frac{1}{2}$ or $\frac{5}{2}$.
>
> Notice, we got $1 \div \frac{2}{5} = \frac{5}{2}$. Checking that with multiplication, we get $\frac{5}{2} \times \frac{2}{5} = 1$. They are reciprocals!

One more example. Thinking of the division problem **1 ÷ (5/7)**, we ask **how many times does 5/7 fit into 1?**

Using pictures: How many times does go into ?

From the picture we can see that goes into just once, and then we have 2/7 left over.

But how many times does $\frac{5}{7}$ fit into the leftover piece, $\frac{2}{7}$? How many times does go into ?

The five-part piece fits into a hole that is only big enough for two parts just 2/5 of the way.

So 5/7 fits into 1 exactly **1 2/5 times**. The division is $1 \div \frac{5}{7} = 1\frac{2}{5}$ or $1 \div \frac{5}{7} = \frac{7}{5}$. Reciprocals again!

5. Solve. Think how many times the given fraction fits into one whole. Write a division.

a. How many times does 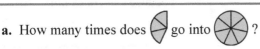 ?

$$1 \div \frac{}{} =$$

b. How many times does go into ?

$$1 \div \frac{}{} =$$

c. How many times does 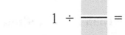 ?

$$1 \div \frac{}{} =$$

d. How many times does go into ?

$$1 \div \frac{}{} =$$

e. How many times does  ?

$$1 \div \frac{}{} =$$

f. How many times does go into ?

$$1 \div \frac{}{} =$$

6. Solve. Think how many times the given fraction fits into the other number. Write a division.

a. How many times does  ?

$$2 \div \frac{}{} =$$

b. How many times does go into ?

$$\frac{}{} \div \frac{}{} =$$

c. How many times does  ?

$$3 \div \frac{}{} =$$

d. How many times does ?

$$\frac{}{} \div \frac{}{} =$$

49

SHORTCUT: instead of dividing, multiply by the reciprocal of the divisor.

Study the examples to see how this works.

How many times does go into ⊕ ?	How many times does ⊗ go into ◯ ⊕ ?	How many times does ✳ go into ✳ ?

$$\frac{3}{4} \div \frac{1}{3}$$

$$\downarrow \quad \downarrow$$

$$\frac{3}{4} \times 3 = \frac{9}{4} = 2\frac{1}{4}$$

Answer: 2 1/4 times.

Does it make sense?

Yes, △ fits into ⊕ a little more than two times.

$$\frac{7}{4} \div \frac{2}{5}$$

$$\downarrow \quad \downarrow$$

$$\frac{7}{4} \times \frac{5}{2} = \frac{35}{8} = 4\frac{3}{8}$$

Answer: 4 3/8 times.

Does it make sense?

Yes. ⊗ goes into 1 3/4 over four times.

$$\frac{2}{9} \div \frac{2}{7} =$$

$$\downarrow \quad \downarrow$$

$$\frac{2}{9} \times \frac{7}{2} = \frac{7}{9}$$

Answer: 7/9 of a time.

Does it make sense?

Yes, because ✳ does not go into ✳ even one full time!

Remember: There are *two* changes in each calculation:

1. **Change the division into multiplication.**
2. **Use the reciprocal of the divisor.**

7. Solve these division problems using the shortcut. Remember to check to make sure your answer makes sense.

a. $\frac{3}{4} \div 5$ $\downarrow \quad \downarrow$ $\frac{3}{4} \times \frac{1}{5} =$	**b.** $\frac{2}{3} \div \frac{6}{7}$
c. $\frac{4}{7} \div \frac{3}{7}$	**d.** $\frac{2}{3} \div \frac{3}{5}$
e. $4 \div \frac{2}{5}$	**f.** $\frac{13}{3} \div \frac{1}{5}$

8. **a.** Write a division to match the situation on the right.

How many times does ⬛⬛⬛⬛⬛ / ⬛⬛⬛⬜ fit into ⬛⬛⬛⬛⬛ ?

We have 8/5, which is eight pieces, trying to fit into five pieces... so they fit 5/8 of the way.

  b. Check your division by multiplication.

9. Fill in.

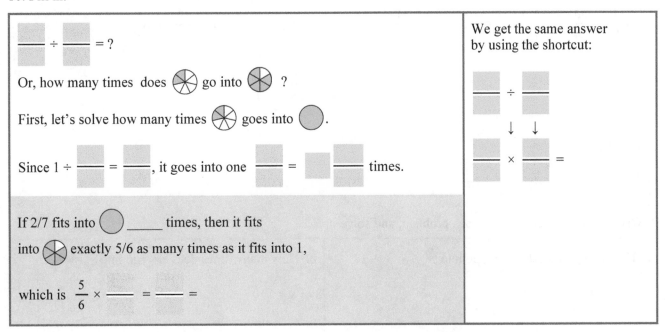

$2 \div \dfrac{3}{4} = ?$

Or, how many times does ⊕ go into ◯ ◯ ?

First, let's solve how many times ⊕ goes into ◯.

Since $1 \div \dfrac{3}{4} = \dfrac{\ \ }{\ \ }$, it goes into one $\dfrac{\ \ }{\ \ } = \boxed{\ \ }\dfrac{\ \ }{\ \ }$ times.

If 3/4 fits into ◯ _____ times, then it fits into ◯◯ **double that many times**, or _____ times.

We get the same answer by using the shortcut:

$2 \div \dfrac{3}{4}$

↓ ↓

$2 \times \dfrac{\ \ }{\ \ } =$

10. Fill in.

$\dfrac{\ \ }{\ \ } \div \dfrac{\ \ }{\ \ } = ?$

Or, how many times does ✳ go into ✳ ?

First, let's solve how many times ✳ goes into ◯.

Since $1 \div \dfrac{\ \ }{\ \ } = \dfrac{\ \ }{\ \ }$, it goes into one $\dfrac{\ \ }{\ \ } = \boxed{\ \ }\dfrac{\ \ }{\ \ }$ times.

If 2/7 fits into ◯ _____ times, then it fits into ✳ exactly 5/6 as many times as it fits into 1,

which is $\dfrac{5}{6} \times \dfrac{\ \ }{\ \ } = \dfrac{\ \ }{\ \ } =$

We get the same answer by using the shortcut:

$\dfrac{\ \ }{\ \ } \div \dfrac{\ \ }{\ \ }$

↓ ↓

$\dfrac{\ \ }{\ \ } \times \dfrac{\ \ }{\ \ } =$

51

Divide Fractions

SHORTCUT: instead of dividing, multiply by the reciprocal of the divisor.

This shortcut works *in every case*, whether the numbers involved are whole numbers or fractions.

$\dfrac{2}{5} \div \dfrac{7}{9}$ ↓ ↓ $\dfrac{2}{5} \times \dfrac{9}{7} = \dfrac{18}{35}$ Check: $\dfrac{18}{35} \times \dfrac{7}{9} = \dfrac{2}{5}$	$7 \div \dfrac{9}{10}$ ↓ ↓ $7 \times \dfrac{10}{9} = \dfrac{70}{9} = 7\dfrac{7}{9}$ Check: $\dfrac{70}{9} \times \dfrac{9}{10} = \dfrac{7}{1} = 7$	$\dfrac{10}{11} \div 5$ ↓ ↓ $\dfrac{10}{11} \times \dfrac{1}{5} = \dfrac{10}{55} = \dfrac{2}{11}$ Check: $\dfrac{2}{11} \times 5 = \dfrac{10}{11}$

Notice: when you check the problems, you will need to use the *original* divisor, not the inverted one.

1. Solve. Change mixed numbers to fractions before dividing. Check each division by multiplication.

a. $\dfrac{9}{10} \div \dfrac{2}{5}$ **Check:**	**b.** $\dfrac{3}{7} \div \dfrac{4}{3}$	**c.** $\dfrac{2}{11} \div \dfrac{2}{3}$
d. $1\dfrac{7}{8} \div \dfrac{3}{4}$ **Check:**	**e.** $2\dfrac{1}{15} \div 1\dfrac{3}{5}$	**f.** $5\dfrac{10}{11} \div 6$

2. Write a division sentence for each problem, and solve it.

a. How many times does  go into ?	**b.** How many times does go into ?

One other meaning of division is **equal sharing**, or "dividing equally between so many people."
In this case, the divisor will be a *whole number*.

Example 1. Divide 8/10 of a pie between four people. Each person gets 2/10. The division is $\dfrac{8}{10} \div 4 = \dfrac{2}{10}$.

Example 2. Solve $\dfrac{6}{7} \div 4$.

We have six slices (each slice being a seventh) and four people. First of all, each person gets one slice and then we have 2 slices left. We split those. So, each person gets 1 1/2 slices. In fraction terms, the 1/2 slice is a fourteenth-part and the 1 slice becomes 2/14. Each person gets a total of 3/14 of the whole.

3. Solve these problems by *reasoning logically.* Write a division sentence for each problem.

a. There is 1 4/6 of a pizza left over and two people share it equally. How much does each person get?	**b.** There is 9/10 of a cake left over and three people share it equally. How much does each person get?

4. The picture shows how much pie is left. That amount is divided among a certain number of people. How much does each person get? Write a division sentence.

a. Divide between three people:	**b.** Share between three people:	**c.** Divide between six people:
d. Divide between two people:	**e.** Divide between five people:	**f.** Share between four people:

5. Three people equally share a 1/4-kg chocolate bar.
   How much chocolate will each of them get?

6. How many 3/8-foot long pieces can you cut out of 11 feet of ribbon?
   How long is the piece that is left over?

7. Five siblings inherited a plot of land that measures 2 4/10 acres.
   If they divide the plot equally, what portion of an acre will each one get?

8. Along with many other ingredients, a recipe calls for 2/3 cup of wheat flour for each batch. In her pantry Sarah had plenty of all the other ingredients, but only a little wheat flour. How many batches of the recipe can she make if she has...

   a. 1/3 cup of wheat flour?

   b. 1 cup of wheat flour?

9. An airport takes up a rectangular area that is 2 1/8 miles long and 1/2 mile wide. What is its area?

10. An airport runway is two miles long, and takes up 1/16 square mile in area. How wide is it, in miles? In feet?

<table>
<tr>
<td>To solve an equation involving fractions, you use the same solution steps as if the equation had whole numbers.

In this case, we divide both sides by 4.</td>
<td>$4x = \dfrac{3}{5}$ $\Big| \div 4$

$x = \dfrac{3}{5} \div 4$

$x = \dfrac{3}{5} \times \dfrac{1}{4} = \dfrac{3}{20}$</td>
</tr>
</table>

11. Solve the equations.

<table>
<tr>
<td>a. $8x = \dfrac{1}{2}$</td>
<td>b. $3x = \dfrac{3}{4}$</td>
</tr>
<tr>
<td>c. $\dfrac{2}{3}x = \dfrac{1}{5}$</td>
<td>d. $\dfrac{2}{3}x = 6$</td>
</tr>
</table>

12. Solve these *easy* division problems!

a. $1 \div \dfrac{3}{4}$	**b.** $1 \div \dfrac{3}{2}$	**c.** $1 \div \dfrac{11}{7}$	**d.** $1 \div 2\dfrac{1}{4}$

13. How many 2/3 cup servings can you get out of 5 cups of ice cream?

14. Sam planted tomatoes in his garden, which is a rectangle with an area of 2 1/2 m². If one side of the garden measures 5 m, how long is the other side?

15. The sides of a rectangle are in a ratio of 2:3, and its perimeter is 1 1/4 inches.

   a. What are the lengths of its sides?

   b. Draw the rectangle.

16. Mary's vegetable garden is 6 1/2 feet by 6 1/2 feet.

   a. Find its area in square feet.

   b. Find its area in square inches.
   (Hint: Change the lengths of the sides into inches.)

   c. Mary divided her garden into quarters in order to plant four different vegetables. What is the area of one of those quarters in square feet?

Problem Solving with Fractions 1

1. The standard letter paper size is 8 1/2 by 11 inches. Let's say you use 1/2-inch margins on all four sides. What is the real printable area of the paper in square inches?

2. **a.** Anna needs to make 30 servings of spiced coffee for a party. Calculate the amount of each ingredient she needs.

> Spiced Coffee – 4 servings
>
> 1 1/2 teaspoons of ground cinnamon
> 1/2 of a teaspoon of ground nutmeg
> 2 tablespoons of sugar
> 1 cup of heavy cream
> 3 cups of coffee
> 4 teaspoons of chocolate syrup

   b. Next week she wants to make just *one* serving for herself. Calculate the amount of each ingredient she needs.

3. Which is a better deal: a $45.55 book at 1/5 off or a $52.80 book at 1/4 off?

Example. Richard paid 3/10 of his $1,140 paycheck in taxes. Of what remained, he paid 1/6 on a loan payment. How much did he have left after those payments?

We will solve this in two steps:

1. First find out how much Richard has left after paying taxes.

2. Then find out how much he has left after paying the loan payment.

1. There are several different ways to find out how much Richard has left after paying taxes:

  (i) We could calculate what 3/10 of $1,140 is, and subtract that from $1,140. First, 1/10 of $1,140 is $114. Then, 3/10 is three times as much, or $342. Lastly, subtract $1,140 − $342 = $798.

  (ii) Since taking away 3/10 of his paycheck leaves 7/10 of it, we could just calculate what 7/10 of $1,140 is. So 1/10 of $1,140 is $114, and 7 × $114 is $798.

  (iii) We could use decimals and calculate 0.7 × $1,140 = $798.

So Richard has $798 left after taxes.

2. His loan payment is 1/6 of $798. We can easily calculate 1/6 of $798 by dividing: $798 ÷ 6 = $133. Subtract that from $798, and we find that Richard has $798 − $133 = $665 left.

4. The unknown is given as a part of a part. Solve for x.

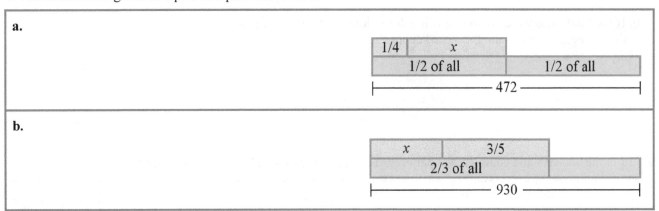

a.

b.

Draw a bar model to help you solve this problem.

5. Elaine gave her grandmother 3/4 of the 48 flowers she had picked.
   Then her grandmother gave 1/4 of *those* flowers to her neighbor.
   How many flowers does Elaine's grandmother have now?
   How many flowers did the neighbor get?
   How many flowers does Elaine have left?

Draw a bar model to help you solve these problems.

6. Dad paid 1/5 of his paycheck in taxes. After that,
   he used 1/6 of what remained as a loan payment.
   Then he had $860 left. How much was his paycheck?

7. Dad used 1/6 of his $1,200 to pay for car repairs.
   Of what was left, he used 2/5 to pay a grocery bill.
   How much money does Dad have left now?

8. **a.** Of the total retail sales of potatoes, the farmer gets 1/8, the wholesale dealer gets 1/12,
   and the store merchant gets the rest. What fraction of the potatoes does the store merchant get?

   b. If the total sales were $4,500, how much (in dollars) would the farmer,
   the wholesale dealer, and the store keeper each get?

9. Fill in the answers and complete the patterns. You'll be able to do a lot of these in your head!

a.	b.	c.	d.
$3 \div \dfrac{1}{5} =$	$6 \div \dfrac{1}{4} =$	$1 \div \dfrac{1}{4} =$	$8 \div \dfrac{1}{2} =$
$3 \div \dfrac{2}{5} =$	$6 \div \dfrac{2}{4} =$	$2 \div \dfrac{1}{4} =$	$8 \div \dfrac{2}{2} =$
$3 \div \dfrac{3}{5} =$	$6 \div \dfrac{3}{4} =$	$3 \div \dfrac{1}{4} =$	$8 \div \dfrac{3}{2} =$
$3 \div \dfrac{4}{5} =$	$\square \div \dfrac{\square}{\square} =$	$\square \div \dfrac{\square}{\square} =$	$\square \div \dfrac{\square}{\square} =$
$3 \div \dfrac{5}{5} =$	$\square \div \dfrac{\square}{\square} =$	$\square \div \dfrac{\square}{\square} =$	$\square \div \dfrac{\square}{\square} =$

Problem Solving with Fractions 2

Example 1. The two sides of a rectangle are in a ratio of 2:3. The perimeter is 7 1/2 inches. How long are the sides?

Let's draw a sketch of the rectangle and mark the sides as 2 and 3 "parts" long. We can see that the perimeter is $2 + 3 + 2 + 3 = 10$ parts long. So, each part is 7 1/2 in ÷ 10. We can find the length

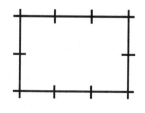

of one part by dividing fractions: $7\frac{1}{2} \div 10 = \frac{15}{2} \times \frac{1}{10} = \frac{3}{4}$.

Remember that 3/4 inch is *not* our final answer! That is just the length of one "part." The short side is 2 parts, so it is 2 × 3/4 in, and the long side is 3 parts, so it is 3 × 3/4 in. Therefore, the sides are 1 1/2 in and 2 1/4 in long.

Check the length of the perimeter: 1 1/2 in + 2 1/4 in + 1 1/2 in + 2 1/4 in = 7 1/2 in, as given.

1. Emily mixed 1 part concentrate with 7 parts water to make a total of 52 ounces of juice. How many ounces of concentrate and how many ounces of water were in the juice?

2. A rectangle has a perimeter of 10 1/2 inches, and its aspect ratio (the ratio of its width to its length) is 1:5. Find the lengths of the two different sides.

3. Heather has two different routes that she can walk to the local swimming pool, and their lengths are in a ratio of 3:4. The shorter route is 1 1/8 miles long. Find the length of the longer route.

Example 2. 2/7 of a class stayed home, so only 25 students showed up at school. How many students are in the whole class?

If 2/7 of the class stayed home, then 5/7 of the class (25 students) came to school. So 25 is 5/7 of the whole group. See the bar model.

We can now solve one "part" (which is 1/7 of the class) by the division $25 \div 5 = 5$.
Therefore, 7/7 of the class — or the whole class — is $7 \times 5 = 35$ students.

4. Fill in the blanks.

a. 3/4 of a number is 15. 1/4 of that number is _____. The number is _____.	**b.** 2/9 of a number is 24. 1/9 of that number is _____. The number is _____.	**c.** 7/8 of a number is 49. 1/8 of that number is _____. The number is _____.

5. Use reasoning similar to what you used in the previous exercise. In each case, find the number.

a. 4/5 of a number is 24.	**b.** 2/3 of a number is 40.
c. 8/11 of a number is 56.	**d.** 5/7 of a number is 45.

6. Of a horse club's members, 7/9 are girls, and 8 (the rest) are boys. How many members does the club have?

7. It took 21 gallons of gas for a tractor to plow 3/5 of a farm. How much gas will be needed to plow the rest of the farm?

8. One-third of the audience at a concert were seniors who had half-price tickets. The total audience count was 657, and a full-price ticket cost $24.50. Find the total income from ticket sales for the concert.
Hint: Start out by finding how many were seniors and how many weren't.

9. Try to visualize this problem by drawing or by using physical objects.

    a. An eraser is 1/8 inch thick. How many erasers
    can be stacked into a 4-inch tall box?

    b. The eraser is 1 3/8 inches long. The box is 6 inches long.
    How many erasers fit in lengthwise?

    c. The eraser is 13/16 inch wide. The box is 5 inches wide.
    How many erasers fit in widthwise?

    d. Use the calculations above to figure out what would be
    the total number of erasers that could fit into the box.

10. How many of the same kind of erasers would fit into a box whose
    dimensions are 12 in (length) by 10 in (width) by 8 in (height)?

11. First, a length of material was cut into two equal
    halves. Then 3/4 of one of the halves was cut off,
    leaving a 17-centimeter piece. How long was
    the material originally?

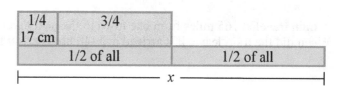

12. Jeremy gave 1/3 of his apple harvest to Dave, who gave half
    of his share to a neighbor. The neighbor got 15.5 kg.
    How many kilograms of apples did Jeremy harvest?

Mixed Review

1. **a.** One mile is 5,280 feet. *Estimate* how many inches are in one mile.

   b. Now *calculate* exactly how many inches are in one mile.

2. Jane mixed 2 parts of concentrated juice with 6 parts of water to make a total of 64 ounces of juice. How many ounces of concentrate and how many ounces of water were in the juice?

3. Write the equivalent rates.

a. $\dfrac{\$80}{4\ \text{hr}} = \dfrac{}{1\ \text{hr}} = \dfrac{}{3\ \text{hr}} = \dfrac{}{15\ \text{min}}$ **b.** $\dfrac{2\ \text{m}^2}{5\ \text{min}} = \dfrac{10\ \text{m}^2}{} = \dfrac{}{5\ \text{hours}} = \dfrac{250\ \text{m}^2}{}$

4. A mixture of salt and water weighs 1.2 kg. It contains 2% salt by weight, and the rest is water. How many grams of salt and how many grams of water are in the mixture?

5. A train traveled 165 miles from one town to the next at an average speed of 90 mph. When did the train leave, if it arrived at 1440 hours (2:40 P.M.)?

6. Multiply or divide the decimals by the powers of ten.

a.	b.	c.
$10 \times 0.3909 =$	$1.08 \times 100 =$	$10^6 \times 8.02 =$
$1{,}000 \times 4.507 =$	$0.0034 \times 10^4 =$	$10^5 \times 0.004726 =$
d.	**e.**	**f.**
$0.93 \div 100 =$	$3.04 \div 1{,}000 =$	$98.203 \div 10^5 =$
$48 \div 10 =$	$450 \div 10^4 =$	$493.2 \div 10^6 =$

7. Factor the following composite numbers into their prime factors.

a. 65 /\	b. 75 /\	c. 82 /\

8. Find a number between 640 and 660 that is divisible by 3 and 7.

9. First, find the GCF of the numbers. Then factor the expressions using the GCF.

a. GCF of 16 and 42 is _____ 16 + 42 = ____ (____ + ____)	b. GCF of 98 and 35 is _____ 98 + 35 = ____ (____ + ____)

10. Draw two rectangles, side by side, to represent the sum 18 + 30.

11. Calculate the values of y according to
    the equation $y = 2x - 5$.

x	3	4	5	6	7	8
y						

Now, plot the points.

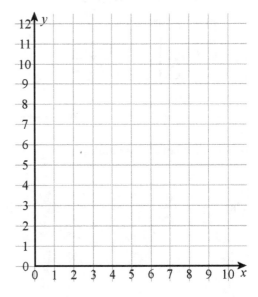

63

Fractions Review

1. Add.

a. $\dfrac{5}{12} + \dfrac{1}{3}$	**b.** $\dfrac{5}{7} + \dfrac{1}{6}$	**c.** $1\dfrac{3}{5} + \dfrac{7}{8}$

2. Subtract. First write equivalent fractions with the same denominator.

a. $\quad 6\dfrac{2}{3} \;\rightarrow$ $\quad - 2\dfrac{1}{6} \;\rightarrow\; -$ —————— ——————	**b.** $\quad 7\dfrac{1}{6} \;\rightarrow$ $\quad - 2\dfrac{3}{5} \;\rightarrow\; -$ —————— ——————	**c.** $\quad 8\dfrac{9}{11} \;\rightarrow$ $\quad - 4\dfrac{1}{3} \;\rightarrow\; -$ —————— ——————

3. The pictures show how much pizza is left. Find the given part of it. Write a multiplication sentence.

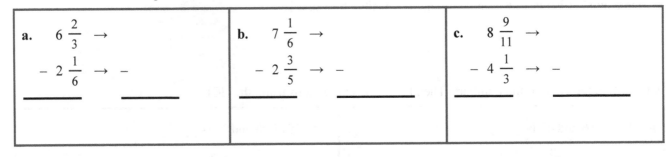

a. Find $\dfrac{3}{4}$ of	**b.** Find $\dfrac{1}{5}$ of	**c.** Find $\dfrac{2}{3}$ of

4. Multiply. Shade the areas to illustrate the multiplication.

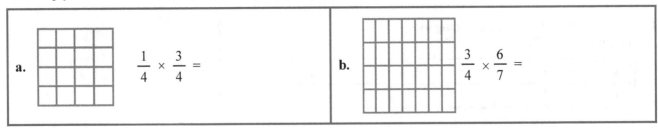

a. $\qquad \dfrac{1}{4} \times \dfrac{3}{4} =$	**b.** $\qquad \dfrac{3}{4} \times \dfrac{6}{7} =$

5. Simplify before you multiply.

a. $\dfrac{9}{12} \times \dfrac{6}{15}$	**b.** $\dfrac{3}{20} \times \dfrac{4}{21}$	**c.** $\dfrac{14}{40} \times \dfrac{10}{42}$

6. Write a division sentence for each problem and solve.

a. How many times does  ?	**b.** How many times does go into ?

7. Fill in the blanks and give an example. You can choose *any* number to divide by 4.

   Dividing a number by 4 is the same as multiplying it by ____. Example:

8. Solve.

a. $\dfrac{2}{3} \div \dfrac{1}{5}$	**b.** $2\dfrac{1}{7} \div 1\dfrac{1}{2}$	**c.** $6 \div 1\dfrac{2}{3}$

9. A small, rectangular garden plot measures 7 1/2 feet by 4 3/8 feet.

   a. Find its area.

   b. Find its perimeter.

10. Write a real-life situation to match this fraction division: $\dfrac{9}{12} \div 3 = \dfrac{3}{12}$

11. How many 4 1/4 inch-pieces can you cut out of a 10-foot piece of string?

12. A 15-inch stick was cut into two pieces that were in the ratio of 1:7.
    How long is each piece?

13. A model airplane is built to a scale of 1:15 compared to the real airplane. This means that the lengths, widths, and other measurements of the real airplane are 15 times as big as the corresponding measurements in the model. If the wingspan of the model is 32 1/4 in, what is the wingspan of the real airplane? Give your answer in feet and inches. *(Hint: You can multiply the whole-number part and the fractional part separately.)*

14. Five-sixths of the class went outside for recess, and 6 students stayed in the classroom.
    How many students are in the whole class?

15. Two-fifths of a certain number is 160. What is the number?

16. Two farmers divided a day's kiwi fruit harvest. One farmer got 2/5 of the harvest and the other farmer got the rest. The farmer who got the least, gave 1/3 of his kiwi to his son, and kept 22 pounds. How many pounds was the day's kiwi fruit harvest?

Puzzle Corner

a. Solve this "long" division!

$$\frac{1}{2} \div 5 \div 4 \div 3 \div 2 =$$

b. What did this division start with?

$$\frac{\quad}{\quad} \div 3 \div 5 \div 7 \div 9 = \frac{1}{1260}$$

Chapter 8: Integers
Introduction

In chapter 8, students are introduced to integers, the coordinate plane in all four quadrants, and integer addition and subtraction. The multiplication and division of integers will be studied in seventh grade.

Integers are introduced using the number line to relate them to the concepts of temperature, elevation, and money. We also study briefly the ideas of absolute value (an integer's distance from zero) and the opposite of a number.

Next, students learn to locate points in all four quadrants and how the coordinates of a figure change when it is reflected across the *x* or *y*-axis. Students also move points according to given instructions and find distances between points with the same first coordinate or the same second coordinate.

Adding and subtracting integers is presented through two main models: (1) movements along the number line and (2) positive and negative counters. With the help of these models, students should not only learn the shortcuts, or "rules," for adding and subtracting integers, but also understand *why* these shortcuts work.

A lesson about subtracting integers explains the shortcut for subtracting a negative integer from three different viewpoints (as a manipulation of counters, as movements on a number line, and as a distance or difference). There is also a roundup lesson for addition and subtraction of integers.

Note: Addition and subtraction of integers are not included in the Common Core standards for sixth grade. I have included them because I feel students are ready to study them, at least to some extent, at the same time as they study the concepts of integers, absolute value, and ordering integers. In seventh grade, we will study all operations with integers.

The last topic in this chapter is graphing. Students will plot points on the coordinate grid according to a given equation in two variables (such as $y = x + 2$), this time using also negative numbers. They will notice the patterns in the coordinates of the points and the pattern in the points drawn in the grid and also work through some real-life problems.

The Lessons in Chapter 8

Helpful Resources on the Internet

CONCEPT OF INTEGERS

Free Integers Video Lessons by Maria
A collection of free video lessons on beginner integers topics for grades 6-9.
http://www.mathmammoth.com/videos/integers/integer_lessons.php

Temperature Comparison
Click on two places on the map, and then compare their average temperatures for a certain month.
http://www.teacherled.com/resources/eurotemps/eurotempsload.html

Interpreting Negative Numbers
Practice explaining the meaning of negative numbers in different scenarios in this interactive exercise.
https://www.khanacademy.org/math/in-sixth-grade-math/integers-india/integers-in/e/negative_number_word_problems

Number Balls Game
Click on the rotating number balls in ascending order.
http://www.sheppardsoftware.com/mathgames/numberballs/numberballsAS2.htm

Order Negative Numbers
Drag and drop the numbers in the right order onto the ladder (scroll down the page a bit to see the activity).
http://www.bbc.co.uk/bitesize/ks3/maths/number/negative_numbers/revision/2/

Number Opposites
Practice finding the opposites of numbers in this online activity from Khan Academy.
https://www.khanacademy.org/math/ab-sixth-grade-math/ab-number/integers-negative-numbers/e/number-opposites

Number Opposites Challenge
Practice solving more challenging problems by finding the opposites of numbers in this online activity.
https://www.khanacademy.org/math/arithmetic-home/negative-numbers/number-opposites/e/opposites-on-the-number-line

Interpreting Absolute Value
Practice understanding the meaning of absolute value in real-world scenarios.
https://www.khanacademy.org/math/algebra-basics/basic-alg-foundations/alg-basics-absolute-value-new/e/absolute-value-word-problems

GRAPHING

Billy Bug Returns
Move Billy Bug to the feeding place with given co-ordinates.
https://www.primarygames.co.uk/pg2/bug2/bug2.html

Graph Mole
A fun game about plotting points in the coordinate plane. Plot the points before the mole eats the vegetables.
http://funbasedlearning.com/algebra/graphing/default.htm

Catch the Fly
Wait for the fly to land on the coordinate grid, then type its coordinates, and a frog will eat it.
http://hotmath.com/hotmath_help/games/ctf/ctf_hotmath.swf

Coordinate Grid Quiz from ThatQuiz.org
This quiz has 10 questions and asks to either plot a point or give the coordinates of a given point. You can also modify the quiz parameters to your liking.
http://www.thatquiz.org/tq-7/?-j8-l5-m2kc0-na-p0

Looking for the Top Quark Game
You receive six quarks that you hide on a grid. Then, use coordinates to find your opponent's hidden quarks.
http://education.jlab.org/topquarkgame

Coordinate Plane Problems
Practice solving word problems by interpreting the meaning of points plotted on an xy co-ordinate system.
https://www.khanacademy.org/math/on-sixth-grade-math/on-geometry-spatial-sense/on-coordinate-plane/e/coordinate-plane-word-problems

Reflecting Points
Practice reflecting points across axes on the xy co-ordinate plane in this interactive online exercise.
https://www.khanacademy.org/math/on-sixth-grade-math/on-geometry-spatial-sense/on-coordinate-plane/e/reflecting-points

Distance Between Two Points
Practice finding the distance between two points on the co-ordinate plane that share the same x or y co-ordinate.
https://www.khanacademy.org/math/ab-sixth-grade-math/shape-space/ab-coordinate-plane/e/relative-position-on-the-coordinate-plane

Desmos Graphing Calculator
A versatile, easy-to-use, and free graphing calculator. To practice plotting points and lines as learned in this chapter, add an item from the "+" button and choose "table." Fill in x and y values, and Desmos will plot the points. You can then type the equation of the line in the form y = (something), such as $y = 2x$, and check if the line goes through your points.
https://www.desmos.com/calculator

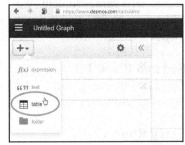

Meta-Calculator 2.0
Choose "Graphing Calculator". You can enter an equation to be graphed, or choose "plot points" from the stop menu to enter individual points.
http://www.meta-calculator.com/online/

Free worksheets for the Coordinate Grid
Generate printable worksheets for plotting points and shapes and for moving and reflecting shapes in the coordinate grid. Options include limiting to the first or all quadrants, scaling, image size, workspace, and border.
http://www.homeschoolmath.net/worksheets/coordinate_grid.php

Graphing Lines Quiz
Improve your graphing skills with this 10-question online quiz.
https://www.thatquiz.org/tq-0/?-j10g-l2-p0

ADDITION AND SUBTRACTION

Number Line Integer Addition
Click on the addition sentence on the fruit that matches the jumps shown on the number line. Choose level 3 to practice concepts studied in this chapter.
http://www.sheppardsoftware.com/mathgames/integers/FS_NumberLine_integer.htm

Number Line Integer Subtraction
Click on the subtraction sentence on the fruit that matches the jumps shown on the number line. Choose level 3 to practice concepts studied in this chapter.
http://www.sheppardsoftware.com/mathgames/integers/FS_NumberLine_int_minus.htm

Number-Line Jump Maker
Use this interactive number-line jump maker tool to practice making jumps of all sizes. Move the slider up or down to change the number line.
http://www.ictgames.com/numberlineJumpMaker/

Temperature Map
Answer questions about temperature in various places using information given to you on a map.
http://mrnussbaum.com/temperature-map-play/

Add Integers Quiz
Practice adding negative and positive numbers in this 10-question online quiz.
https://www.thatquiz.org/tq-1/?-j4101-la-p0

Integers Conundrum
Can you solve the conundrum? Each number is the sum of the two numbers directly beneath it.
http://www.mathplayground.com/number_conundrum/number_conundrum_integers.html

Integer Tilt
Use the arrow keys to guide the falling blocks to the side that they need to land on in order to keep the bar balanced.
http://www.hoodamath.com/games/integertilt2.html

Integer War Card Game
In this card game, students work in pairs to compare integers, as well as add, subtract, or multiply, depending on which operation is being practiced.
http://www.mathfilefoldergames.com/integer-war/

Red and Black TripleMatch Game for Adding Integers
This is a fun card game for 2-5 people to practice adding integers.
http://mathmamawrites.blogspot.com/2010/07/black-and-red-triplematch-card-game-for.html

Casey Runner
See if you can help Casey reach the finish line by correctly adding or subtracting negative and positive numbers.
http://www.mathsisfun.com/numbers/casey-runner.html

Subtract Integers Quiz
Practice subtracting integers in this interactive 10-question quiz.
https://www.thatquiz.org/tq-1/?-j4102-lc-p0

Missing Numbers Quiz
Find the missing numbers in this 10-question quiz that practices addition and subtraction of integers.
https://www.thatquiz.org/tq-1/?-j113-lc-p0

GENERAL

Create Integers Worksheets
Use the basic operations worksheet generator to make worksheets for integers within a certain range of negative to positive numbers.
http://www.homeschoolmath.net/worksheets/basic-operations-worksheets.php

Free Downloadable Integer Fact Sheets
http://www.homeschoolmath.net/download/Add_Subtract_Integers_Fact_Sheet.pdf
http://www.homeschoolmath.net/download/Multiply_Divide_Integers_Fact_Sheet.pdf

The History of Negative Numbers
Although they seem normal to us now, in the past negative numbers have spurred controversy and been called "fictitious" or worse.
http://nrich.maths.org/5961
http://www.classzone.com/books/algebra_1/page_build.cfm?content=links_app3_ch2&ch=2

Integers

When we continue the number line towards the left from zero, we come to the **negative numbers**.

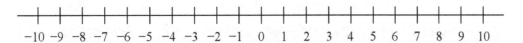

The **negative whole numbers** are −1, −2, −3, −4, and so on.
The **positive whole numbers** are 1, 2, 3, 4, and so on. You can also write them as +1, +2, +3, *etc.*
Zero is neither positive nor negative.
All of the negative and positive whole numbers and zero are called **integers**.

Read −1 as "negative one" and −5 as "negative five." Some people read −5 as "minus five."
That is very common, and it is not wrong, but be sure that you do not confuse it with subtraction.

Put a "−" sign in front of negative numbers. This sign can also be elevated: ⁻5 is the same as −5.

Often, we need to put parentheses around negative numbers in order to avoid confusion with other symbols.
Therefore, ⁻5, −5, and (−5) all mean "negative five."

Negative numbers are commonly used with temperature. They are also used to express debt. If you owe
$5, you write that as −$5. Another use is with elevation below sea level. For example, just as 200 m can
mean an elevation of 200 meters above sea level, −100 m would mean 100 meters *below* sea level.

1. Plot the integers on the number line.

      a. −7   **b.** +6   **c.** −4   **d.** −2

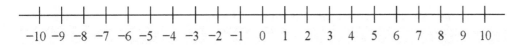

2. Write an integer appropriate to each situation.

   a. Daniel owes $23.

   b. Mary earned $250.

   c. The airplane flew at the altitude of 8,800 meters.

   d. The temperature in the freezer is 18 degrees Celsius below zero.

   e. A dolphin dove 30 ft below sea level.

3. The temperature changed from what it was before. Find the new temperature.
   You can draw the mercury on the thermometer to help you.

before	1°C	2°C	−2°C	−4°C	−12°C	−8°C
change	drops 3°C	drops 7°C	drops 1°C	rises 5°C	rises 4°C	rises 3°C
now						

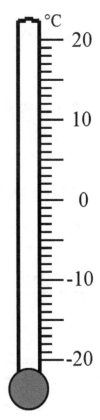

71

Which is more, −5 or −2?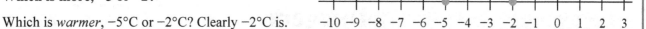

Which is *warmer*, −5°C or −2°C? Clearly −2°C is.
Temperatures just get colder and colder the more
you move towards the negative numbers. We can write a comparison: −2°C > −5°C.

Which is the *better* money situation, to have −$5 (owe $5) or to have −$2 (owe $2)?
Clearly, it is better to owe only $2 because you can pay that off easier. We can write: −$5 < −$2.

Which is the *higher* elevation, −5 m or −2 m? Of course, 2 m below sea level, or −2m, is higher.

On the number line, the number that is ***farther to the right*** is the **greater** number. So, −5 < −2.

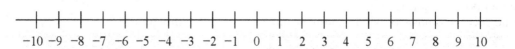

4. Compare. Write < or > between the numbers. You can plot the integers on the number line to help you.

a. −2 ☐ −3	**b.** 8 ☐ −8	**c.** −3 ☐ 0	**d.** 4 ☐ −3	**e.** −5 ☐ −9
f. −10 ☐ −30	**g.** −4 ☐ 1	**h.** 0 ☐ −13	**i.** −2 ☐ −7	**j.** −11 ☐ −14

5. You can use the number line to help you. Which integer is ...

   a. 2 more than −4   **b.** 5 more than −3   **c.** 3 less than 1   **d.** 6 more than −11

6. Find the number that is 5 less than ...   **a.** 0   **b.** −3   **c.** 3

7. Express the situations using integers. Then write > or < to compare them.

   a. Shelly owes $10 and Mary owes $8.

   b. Mommy fish was swimming 3 m below the surface of the water,
      and Daddy fish was swimming 4 m below the surface of the water.

   c. The temperature this morning was 10°C below zero. Now it is 6°C below zero.

   d. Henry has $5. Emma owes $5.

   e. The temperature during the day was 10°C but at night it was 2°C below zero.

8. Write the numbers in order from the least to the greatest.

a. −2 0 −4 4	**b.** −3 −6 5 3
c. −20 −10 −14 −9	**d.** −3 0 −6 −8

The **absolute value** of a number is its distance from zero.

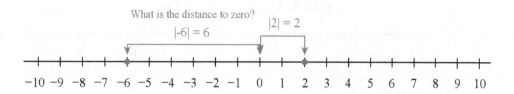

We denote the absolute value of a number using vertical bars around the number.

So, $|-4|$ means "the absolute value of 4," which is 4. Similarly, $|87| = 87$.

9. Find the absolute values of these numbers.

    a. $|-5|$ **b.** $|-12|$ **c.** $|7|$ **d.** $|0|$ **e.** $|68|$

The **opposite** of a number is the number that is at the same distance from zero as it is, but on the *opposite* side of the number line (in regards to zero).

The opposite of −7 is 7.
$-(-7) = 7$

−10 −9 −8 −7 −6 −5 −4 −3 −2 −1 0 1 2 3 4 5 6 7 8 9 10

We denote the opposite of a number using the minus sign. For example, −4 means the opposite of 4, which is negative four. Or, −(−2) means the opposite of negative two, which is 2.

The opposite of zero is zero itself. In symbols, −0 = 0.

"But wait," you might ask, "doesn't −4 mean negative four, not the 'opposite of four'?"

The funny thing is, −4 can mean either. ☺ Sometimes the context will help you to tell which is which. Other times it's unnecessary to differentiate because, after all, the opposite of four *is* negative four: −4 = −4.

So there are three different meanings for the minus sign:

1. To indicate subtraction: $7 - 2 = 5$.
2. To indicate negative numbers: "negative 7" is written −7.
3. To indicate the opposite of a number: −(−14) is the opposite of negative 14.

10. Think of the minus sign as signifying "the opposite of". Simplify.

    a. −5   **b.** −(−9)   **c.** −10   **d.** −0   **e.** −(−100)

11. Write using mathematical symbols, and simplify (solve) if possible.

    a. the opposite of 6   **d.** the absolute value of the opposite of 6

    b. the opposite of the absolute value of 6   **e.** the opposite of −6.

    c. the absolute value of negative 6   **f.** the absolute value of the opposite of −6

Coordinate Grid

This is the *coordinate grid* or *coordinate plane*. We have extended the *x*-axis and the *y*-axis to include negative numbers now. The axes cross each other at the *origin*, or the point (0, 0).

The axes divide the coordinate plane into four parts, called *quadrants*. Previously you have worked in only the so-called first quadrant, but now we will use all four quadrants.

The coordinates of a point are found in the same manner as before. Draw a vertical line (either up or down) from the point towards the *x*-axis. Where this line crosses the *x*-axis tells you the point's *x*-coordinate.

Similarly, draw a horizontal line (either right or left) from the point towards the *y*-axis. Where this line crosses the *y*-axis tells you the point's *y*-coordinate.

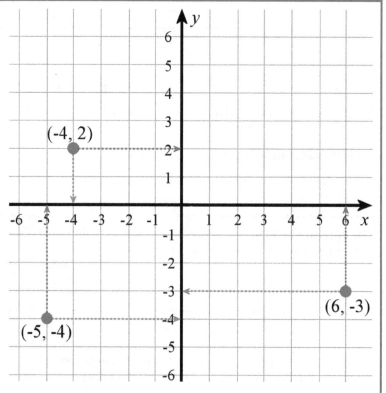

We list first the point's *x*-coordinate and then the *y*-coordinate. Look at the examples in the picture.

1. Write the *x*- and *y*-coordinates of the points.

A (____ , ____)

B (____ , ____)

C (____ , ____)

D (____ , ____)

E (____ , ____)

F (____ , ____)

G (____ , ____)

Self-check: Add the x-coordinates of all points. You should get −7.

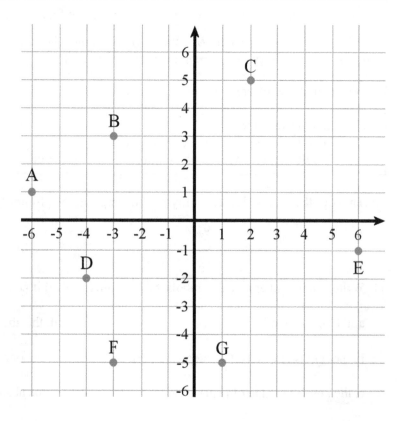

74

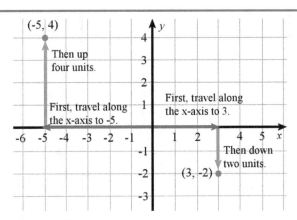

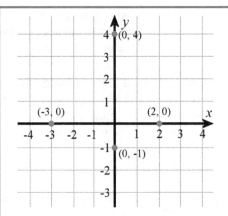

How to plot a point

1. First travel along the *x*-axis to the number of the *x*-coordinate.

2. Travel *up or down* the number of units of the *y*-coordinate.

   Naturally, if the *y*-coordinate is positive, you travel up. If it is negative, you travel down.

Remember:

If the point is <u>on</u> the *x*-axis, then its *y*-coordinate is zero.

If the point is <u>on</u> the *y*-axis, then its *x*-coordinate is zero.

2. Plot the following sets of points. Connect them with line segments to form figures. Which figures are formed?

a. (−2, 4), (2, 4), (−2, 0), (2, 0)

b. (−6, −6), (−5, −5), (−2, −5), (−3, −6)

c. (2, −5), (3, −2), (5, −2), (8, −5)

d. (−6, 0), (−3, 4), (0, 0)

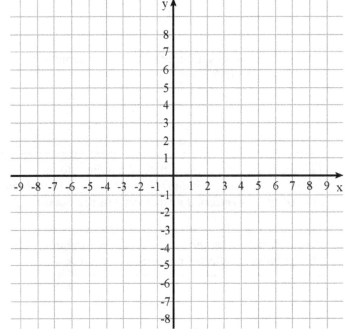

3. Find the area of the rectangle whose vertices are at (−1, 6), (−1, −2), (3, −2), and (3, 6).

4. Two vertices of a rectangle are (−5, −3) and (−2, 4). What are the other two vertices?

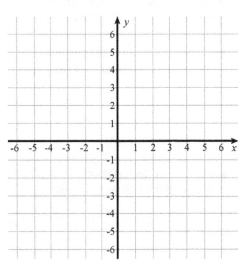

75

5. **a.** Plot the following points: (−6, 5), (−5, 3), (−3, 3), (−1, 4), (−2, 5). Then connect the points with line segments in the order they are given.

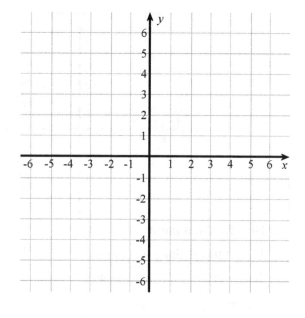

   b. For each point above, **change the x-coordinate into its opposite.** That means that −5 changes to 5, −1 changes to 1, and so on. Do not change the y-coordinates. Write the points here:

   c. Plot these new points. Connect them in the same order. What do you notice?

6. For each of these points (−6, 5), (−5, 3), (−3, 3), (−1, 4), (−2, 5), **change the y-coordinate into its opposite.**

   Plot these new points. Connect them in the same order. What do you notice?

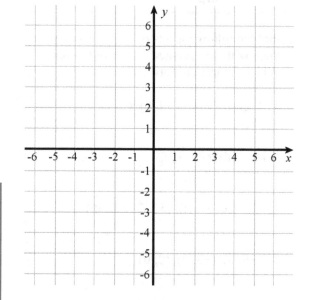

When we change the x-coordinate of a point into its opposite, without changing the y-coordinate (as in problem 5), the point gets *reflected* or *mirrored* **in the y-axis.**

When we change the y-coordinate of a point into its opposite, without changing the x-coordinate (as in problem 6), the point gets *reflected* or *mirrored* **in the x-axis.**

7. **a.** The vertices of a shape are (−6, 2), (−2, 2), (−4, 6), and (4, 6). Draw the shape.

   b. Reflect the points in the x-axis. Write the coordinates of the points here.

   c. Join the reflected points in order to form a new shape. What is it called?

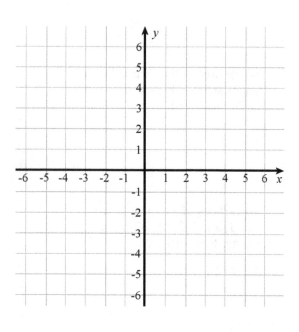

8. Reflect these points in the *x*-axis. What are the coordinates of the reflected points?

    a. (2, 7)   **b.** (−15, 20)   **c.** (−11, −21)   **d.** (34, −19)

9. Reflect these points in the *y*-axis. What are the coordinates of the reflected points?

    a. (3, 9)   **b.** (22, −20)   **c.** (−67, −35)   **d.** (−51, 60)

10. **a.** Draw a trapezoid with vertices of (4, 2), (7, 2), (8, 6), and (5, 6).

    b. Now mirror it in the *y*-axis.

    c. Reflect the same, original trapezoid in the *x*-axis.

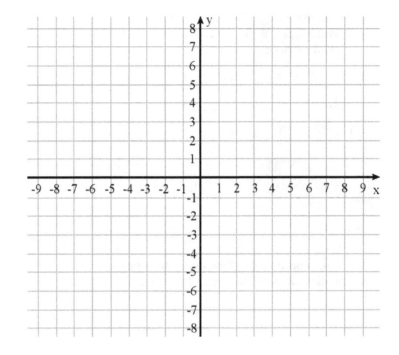

11. The points (−2, 1), (−8, 2), (−6, 3), (−8, 4), and (−2, 5) are the vertices of a pennant.

    a. Draw the pennant.

    b. Reflect it in the *y*-axis.

    c. After reflecting it, now move the pennant five units down.

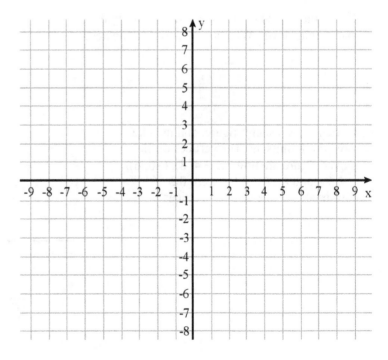

Puzzle Corner

Anne drew a secret figure. She moved it 2 units up, and then she mirrored it in the *x*-axis. Its vertices are now at: (−7, −7), (−4, −3), and (−2, −6). What were the coordinates of the original vertices?

Coordinate Grid Practice

Notice in the grid, the point (−6, 5) moves four units to the right. It ends up at (−2, 5).

1. **a.** The points (−5, −2), (−1, −7), and (1, −6) are vertices of a triangle. Draw the triangle.

   b. Move the triangle five units up (draw the new triangle). Write the coordinates of the moved vertices.

   (−5, −2) → (_____ , _____)

   (−1, −7) → (_____ , _____)

   (1, −6) → (_____ , _____)

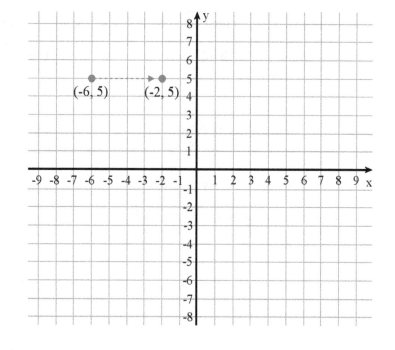

2. Write the coordinates of the new points based on the directions in the box on the right.

Point	Direction	New point
(1, 1)	7 units down	
(2, −2)	6 units left	
(−2, 7)	5 units right	
(−2, −2)	4 units down	

3. The point (−5, 5) is moved 8 units to the right *and* 3 units down. What are its new coordinates?

4. Jayden drew a secret figure, and then he moved it 8 units up. The vertices of the moved figure are now at: (−4, 8), (−6, 6), (−4, 2), and (1, 6). What were the coordinates of the original vertices?

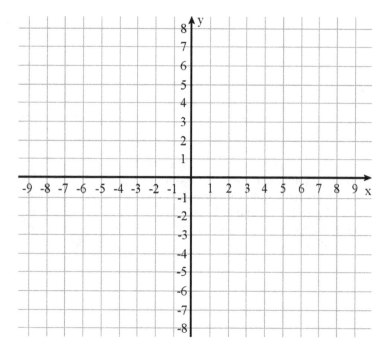

5. Find the difference between the two temperatures. You can use the thermometer to help you.

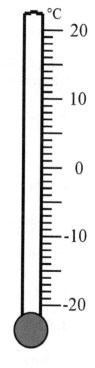

a. −3°C and 3°C

b. 4°C and −6°C

c. −15°C and −7°C

d. −4°C and 12°C

e. −7°C and −28°C

f. −3°C and 0°C

g. 6°C and −6°C

h. 0°C and −13°C

6. *Explain* in your own words how to find the **distance** between the numbers −29 and 28 on a number line.

7. Change your explanation above (if need be) so that you use *absolute value* in your explanation.

8. *Explain* in your own words how to find the distance between two negative numbers, such as −49 and −72, on the number line.

To find the distance between two numbers where one is negative and the other is positive, add their absolute values. Remember, the absolute value tells us how far the number is from zero.

Example 1. The distance between −99 and 99 is $|-99| + |99|$ or $99 + 99 = 198$.

To find the distance between two negative numbers, you can simply find the distance between their opposites, which are both positive numbers.

Example 2. The distance between −1,200 and −500 is the same as the distance between 1,200 and 500, which is 700 (you can subtract $1200 - 500$ to find that).

---

9. Find the distances between the points.

a. (12, 56) and (12, −15)

b. (−34, 9) and (−8, 9)

10. Find the perimeter of a rectangle with vertices (46, 50), (−22, 50), (−22, −17), and (46, −17).

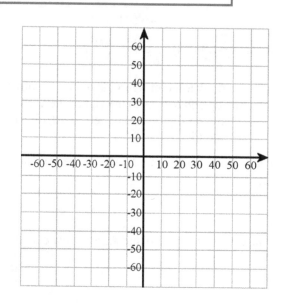

11. Lily drew a map of her neighborhood. She put her house at the origin, or the point (0, 0). Each square on the map is **50 ft**.

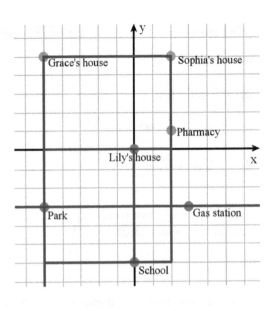

What are the coordinates of...
(Remember that the gridlines are 50 ft apart.)

a. ...the school?

b. ...Grace's house?

c. ...the park?

Find the distances:

d. from the park to the gas station.

e. Sophia's house to Grace's house.

f. What is the distance from (−200, 100) to (−25, 100)?

g. What is the distance from (−300, 250) to (−300, −350)?

12. Activity (optional). Use a street map of any town where the streets are in a grid. Print it out and draw a coordinate grid with all four quadrants over it. Now, make a treasure hunt or a similar activity for your friend, giving locations using coordinates or using directions (go such-and-such a distance left, right, up, down, or north, south, east, west).

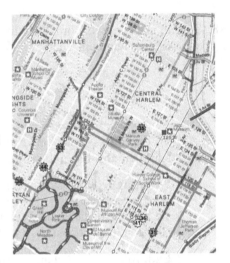

Puzzle Corner

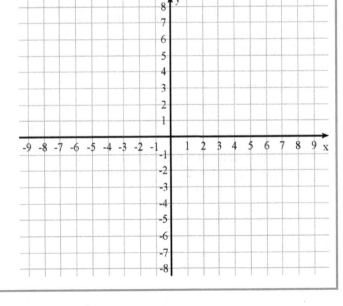

Aaron drew a secret figure, and then he moved it 2 units up and 6 units to the right. The vertices of the moved figure are now at: (0, 0), (3, 5), (5, 0), and (8, 5).

a. What were the coordinates of the original vertices?

b. What is the figure that Aaron drew called?

Addition and Subtraction as Movements

Suppose you are at 4. You jump 5 steps *to the right*. You end up at 9. We write <u>*an addition*</u>: $4 + 5 = 9$.

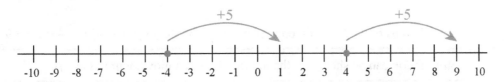

Now you are at −4. You jump 5 steps *to the right*. You end up at 1. We write <u>*an addition*</u>: $-4 + 5 = 1$.

Addition can be shown on the number line as a movement to the *right*.

1. Write an addition sentence (an equation) to match each of the number line jumps.

a.

b.

c.

d.

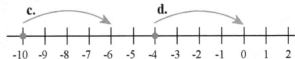

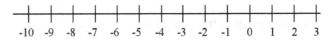

2. Draw a number line jump for each addition sentence.

a. $-8 + 2 =$ _____   **b.** $-5 + 4 =$ _____

c. $-7 + 5 =$ _____   **d.** $-10 + 12 =$ _____

3. Write an addition sentence.

Addition sentence:

a. You are at ¯3. You jump 6 to the right. You end up at _____.

b. You are at ¯8. You jump 8 to the right. You end up at _____.

c. You are at ¯4. You jump 7 to the right. You end up at _____.

d. You are at ¯10. You jump 3 to the right. You end up at _____.

You are at 4. You jump 5 steps *to the left*. You end up at −1. We write <u>*a subtraction*</u>: $4 - 5 = -1$.

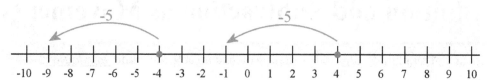

You are at −4. You jump 5 steps *to the left*. You end up at −9. We write <u>*a subtraction*</u>: $-4 - 5 = -9$.

Subtraction can be shown on the number line as a movement to the *left*.

Note: These three mean the same:

$-4 - 5 = -9$ We can use parentheses around a negative number if we need to make clear that the minus sign is for "negative," and not for subtraction. We can also use an elevated minus sign for clarity. However, in the above situation, there is no confusion, so the parentheses are not necessary and are usually omitted.

$(-4) - 5 = (-9)$

$^-4 - 5 = {}^-9$

4. Write a subtraction sentence to match the number line jumps.

a.

b.

c.

d.

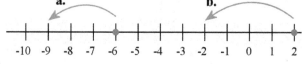

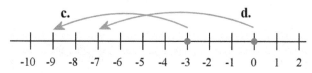

5. Draw a number line jump for each subtraction.

a. $1 - 5 =$ _____   **b.** $0 - 8 =$ _____

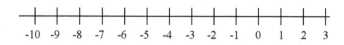

c. $-2 - 4 =$ _____   **d.** $-7 - 3 =$ _____

6. Write a subtraction sentence.   Subtraction sentence:

    a. You are at $^-3$. You jump 5 to the left. You end up at _____.

    b. You are at 5. You jump 10 to the left. You end up at _____.

    c. You are at $^-5$. You jump 5 to the left. You end up at _____.

Number line jumps with mixed addition and subtraction

- The first number tells you where you *start*.
- Next comes the sign: a *plus* sign tells you to jump *right*, and a *minus* sign tells you to jump *left*.
- Next comes the number of *steps* to jump.

Notice that the number of steps that you jump is *not* negative.

−2 + 6 means: Start at −2 and move 6 steps to the right. You end up at 4. You started out negative, but you moved towards the positives, and you ended up on the positive side!	−2 − 6 means: Start at −2 and move 6 steps to the left. You end up at −8. You started out negative at −2 and ended up even more negative at −8.

7. Add or subtract. Think of the number line jumps.

a. $3 - 4 =$ $2 - 5 =$ $5 - 9 =$	**b.** $^-2 - 1 =$ $^-6 - 4 =$ $^-7 - 2 =$	**c.** $^-4 + 4 =$ $^-7 + 3 =$ $^-12 + 5 =$	**d.** $^-5 + 6 =$ $^-8 + 4 =$ $^-6 + 7 =$

8. Find the number that is missing from the equations. Think of moving on the number line.

a. $1 - \underline{\hspace{1cm}} = {}^-4$ **b.** $3 - \underline{\hspace{1cm}} = {}^-3$	**c.** $^-7 + \underline{\hspace{1cm}} = {}^-6$ **d.** $^-9 + \underline{\hspace{1cm}} = {}^-1$	**e.** $2 - \underline{\hspace{1cm}} = {}^-5$ **f.** $0 - \underline{\hspace{1cm}} = {}^-8$	**g.** $^-3 + \underline{\hspace{1cm}} = 0$ **h.** $^-9 + \underline{\hspace{1cm}} = 9$

9. The expression $1 - 2 - 3 - 4$ can also be thought of as a person making jumps on the number line. Where does the person end up?

10. James had $5. He bought coffee for $2 and a sandwich for $6. He paid what he could and the cashier put the rest of the bill on his charge account with the store.

   a. Write a math sentence to show the transaction.

   b. How much in debt is James now?

What about adding or subtracting a negative number?

Here is a way to think about $3 - (-2)$. Imagine you are standing at 3 to start with. Because of the subtraction sign, you turn to the left and get ready to take your steps. However, because of the additional minus sign in front of the 2, you have to take those steps BACKWARD—to the right! So, because you ended up taking those 2 steps to the *right*, in effect, you have just performed $3 + 2$.

Another example: Here is a way to think about $-4 + (-5)$. Imagine you are standing at −4 to start with. Because of the addition sign, you turn to the right and get ready to move. But because of the additional minus sign in front of the 5, you have to take those 5 steps BACKWARD. So you take those 5 steps to the *left* instead. In essence, you have performed $-4 - 5$. (In the next lesson we will examine *other* ways to think about these situations.)

Adding Integers: Counters

Addition of integers can be modeled using **counters**. We will use green counters with a "+" sign for positives and red counters with a "−" sign for negatives.

Here we have the sum 2 + 3. There is a group of 2 positives and another of 3 positives.

This picture shows the sum (−2) + (−3). We *add* negatives and negatives. In total, there are five negatives, so the sum is −5.

$$1 + (-1) = 0$$

One positive counter and one negative counter *cancel* each other. In other words, their sum is zero!

$$2 + (-2) = 0$$

Two negatives and two positives also cancel each other. Their sum is zero.

$$3 + (-1) = 2$$

Here, one "positive-negative" pair is canceled (you can cross it out!). We are left with 2 positives.

$$(-4) + 3 = -1$$

Now the negatives outweigh the positives. Pair up three negatives with three positives. Those cancel out. There is still one negative left.

1. Refer to the pictures and add. Remember each "positive-negative" pair is canceled.

 a. 2 + (−5) = _____	 **b.** (−3) + 5 = _____	 **c.** (−6) + (−3) = _____
 d. 3 + (−5) = _____	 **e.** 2 + (−4) = _____	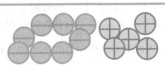 **f.** (−8) + 5 = _____

2. Write addition sentences (equations) to match the pictures.

 a.	 **b.**	 **c.**
 d.	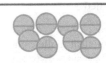 **e.**	 **f.**

A note on notation

We can write an elevated minus sign to indicate a negative number: ⁻4.
Or we can write it with a minus sign and parentheses: (−4).
We can even write it without the parentheses if the meaning is clear: −4.

So ⁻4 + ⁻4 = ⁻8 is the same as (−4) + (−4) = (−8), which is the same as −4 + (−4) = −8.

You *should* write the parentheses if you have + and −, or two − signs, next to each other.

So, do *not* write "8 + − 4"; write "8 + (−4)." And do not write "3 − −3"; write "3 − (−3)."

3. Think of the counters. Add.

a. 7 + (−8) = (−7) + 8 =	**b.** (−7) + (−8) = 7 + 8 =	**c.** 5 + (−7) = 7 + (−5) =	**d.** 50 + (−20) = 10 + (−40) =
e. ⁻2 + ⁻4 = ⁻6 + 6 =	**f.** 10 + ⁻1 = ⁻10 + ⁻1 =	**g.** ⁻8 + 2 = ⁻8 + ⁻2 =	**h.** ⁻9 + ⁻1 = 9 + ⁻1 =

4. Rewrite these sentences using symbols, and solve the resulting sums.

    a. The sum of seven positives and five negatives.

    b. Add −3 and −11.

    c. Positive 100 and negative 15 added together.

5. Write a sum for each situation and solve it.

    a. Your checking account is overdrawn by $50. (This means your account is negative).
       Then you deposit $60. What is the balance in your account now?

    b. Hannah owed $20 to her mom. Then, she borrowed $15 more from her mom.
       What is Hannah's "balance" now?

6. Consider the four expressions 2 + 6, (−2) + (−6), (−2) + 6, and 2 + (−6). Write these
   expressions in order from the one with **least** value to the one with **greatest** value.

7. Find the number that is missing from the equations.

a. −3 + _____ = −7	**b.** −3 + _____ = 3	**c.** 3 + _____ = (−7)
d. _____ + (−15) = −22	**e.** 2 + _____ = −5	**f.** _____ + (−5) = 0

Comparing number line jumps and counters

We can think of $-5 + (-3)$ as five negatives and three negatives, totaling 8 negatives or -8. We also know that $-5 - 3$ is like starting at -5 and jumping three steps towards the left on the number line, ending at -8.

Since both have the same answer, the two expressions $-5 + (-3)$ and $-5 - 3$ are equal:

$$-5 + (-3) = -5 - 3$$

It is as if the "$+ -$" in the middle is changed into a single $-$ sign. This, indeed, is a *shortcut*!

Similarly, $2 + (-7)$ is the same as $2 - 7$. Either (1) think of having 2 positive and 7 negative counters, totaling 5 negatives, (2) or think of being at 2 and taking 7 steps to the left, ending at -5.

When solving integer problems, you can think of number line jumps or of counters, whichever is easier.

8. Compare how $-7 + 4$ is modeled on the number line and with counters.

   a. On the number line, $-7 + 4$ is like starting at _____, and moving _____ steps to the _____, ending at _____.

   b. With counters, $-7 + 4$ is like _____ negatives and _____ positives added together. We can form _____ negative-positive pairs that cancel, and what is left is _____ negatives.

9. Add.

a. $4 + (-10) =$	**b.** $-8 + (-8) =$	**c.** $-5 + (-7) =$	**d.** $11 + (-2) =$
$-6 + 8 =$	$7 + (-8) =$	$12 + (-5) =$	$-10 + 20 =$

10. **a.** Find the value of the expression $x + (-4)$ for four different values of x. You can choose the values.

   b. For which value of x does the expression $x + (-4)$ have the value 0?

11. Solve the problems, and observe the patterns.

a. $3 - 2 =$	**b.** $^-7 - 0 =$	**c.** $^-5 + 0 =$	**d.** $^-6 + 6 =$
$3 - 3 =$	$^-7 - 1 =$	$^-5 + 1 =$	$^-6 + 7 =$
$3 - 4 =$	$^-7 - 2 =$	$^-5 + 2 =$	$^-6 + 8 =$
$3 - 5 =$	$^-7 - 3 =$	$^-5 + 3 =$	$^-6 + 9 =$
$3 - 6 =$	$^-7 - 4 =$	$^-5 + 4 =$	$^-6 + 10 =$

Subtracting a Negative Integer

We have already looked at such subtractions as $3 - 5$ or $-2 - 8$, which you can think of as number line jumps. But what about **subtracting a negative integer?** What is $5 - (-4)$? Or $(-5) - (-3)$?

Let's look at this kind of expression with a "double negative" in several different ways.

1. Subtraction as "taking away":

We can model subtracting a negative number using counters. $(-5) - (-3)$ means we start with 5 negative counters, and then we *take away* 3 negative counters. That leaves 2 negatives, or -2.

$5 - (-4)$ cannot easily be modeled that way, because it is hard to take away 4 negative counters when we do not have any negative counters to start with. But you *could* do it this way:

Start out with 5 positives. Then *add* four positive-negative pairs, which is just adding zero! Now you can take away four negatives. You are left with nine positives.

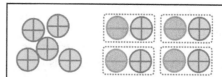

Start out with 5. Add four positive-negative pairs, which amount to zero.

Lastly, cross out four negatives. You are left with nine positives.

2. Subtracting a negative number as a number line jump:

$5 - (-4)$ is like standing at 5 on the number line, and getting ready to subtract, or go to the left. But, since there is a minus sign in front of the 4, it "turns you around" to face the positive direction (to the right), and you take 4 steps to the right instead. So, $5 - (-4) = 5 + 4 = 9$.

$(-5) - (-3)$ is like standing at -5, ready to go to the left, but the minus sign in front of 3 turns you "about face," and you take 3 steps to the right instead. You end up at -2.

3. Subtraction as a difference/distance:

To find the difference between 76 and 329, you subtract $329 - 76 = 253$ (the smaller-valued number from the bigger-valued one). If you subtract the numbers the other way, $76 - 329$, the answer is -253.

By the same analogy, we can think of $5 - (-4)$ as meaning the difference (distance) between 5 and -4. From the number line we can see the distance is **9**.

$(-5) - (-3)$ *could* be the distance between -5 and -3, except it has the larger number, -3, subtracted from the smaller number, -5.

If we turn them around, $(-3) - (-5)$ would give us the distance (difference) between those two numbers, which is 2. Then, $(-5) - (-3)$ would be the opposite of that, or -2.

Two negatives make a positive!

You have probably already noticed that, any way you look at it, we can, in effect, replace those two minuses in the middle with a + sign. In other words, $5 - (-4)$ has the same answer as $5 + 4$. And $(-5) - (-3)$ has the same answer as $-5 + 3$. It may look a bit strange, but it works out really well.

$$5 - (-4)$$
$$5 + 4 = 9$$

$$(-5) - (-3)$$
$$(-5) + 3 = -2$$

1. Write a subtraction sentence to match the pictures.

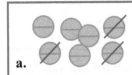

a.

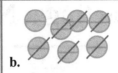

b.

2. Write an addition or subtraction sentence to match the number line movements.

    a. You are at −2. You jump 6 steps to the left.

    b. You are at −2. You get ready to jump 6 steps to the left,
        but turn around at the last minute and jump 6 steps to the right instead.

3. Find the distance between the two numbers. Then, write a matching subtraction sentence. To get a positive
   distance, remember to *subtract the <u>smaller</u> number from the <u>bigger</u> number.*

a. The distance between 3 and −7 is _____.	**b.** The distance between −3 and −9 is _____.
Subtraction: _____ − _____ = _____	Subtraction: _____ − _____ = _____
c. The distance between −2 and 10 is _____.	**d.** The distance between −11 and −20 is _____.
Subtraction: _____ − _____ = _____	Subtraction: _____ − _____ = _____

4. Solve. Remember the shortcut: you can change each double minus "− −" into a plus sign.

a. $-8 - (-4) =$	**b.** $-1 - (-5) =$	**c.** $12 - (-15) =$
$8 - (-4) =$	$1 - (-5) =$	$-12 + 15 =$
$-8 + (-4) =$	$-1 - 5 =$	$-12 - 15 =$
$8 + (-4) =$	$1 - 5 =$	$12 + (-15) =$

5. Connect with a line the
   expressions that are equal
   (have the same value).

	a.		**b.**	
$10 - (-3)$	$10 - 3$	$-9 + 2$	$-9 + (-2)$
$10 + (-3)$	$10 + 3$	$-9 - 2$	$-9 - (-2)$

6. Write an integer addition or subtraction to describe the situations.

    a. A roller coaster begins at 90 ft above ground level.
        Then it descends 105 feet.

    b. Matt has $25. He wants to buy a bicycle from his friend that costs $40.
        How much will he owe his friend?

Solve $-1 + (-2) - (-3) - 4$.

Puzzle Corner

Add and Subtract Roundup

1. Addition of integers.

- Think of positive and negative counters.

- When adding a negative and positive integer, you can also think of number line jumps.

Example 1. $-4 + 11$	**Example 2.** $-4 + (-11)$
a. Think of a number line: you are at -4 and jump 11 steps to the right. You end up at 7.	**b.** Think of 4 negative and 11 negative counters. The negatives add up, giving us -15.

	Example 3. $4 + (-11)$
b. Think of 4 negative and 11 positive counters. Four negative-positive pairs cancel each other, and 7 positives are left.	**b.** Think of 4 positive and 11 negative counters. Four negative-positive pairs cancel each other, and 7 negatives are left.

1. Addition skills check-up! Add.

a. $-4 + 6 =$ _____	**b.** $-3 + 7 =$ _____	**c.** $8 + (-9) =$ _____
$4 + (-6) =$ _____	$-3 + (-7) =$ _____	$(-8) + (-9) =$ _____

2. Subtraction of integers.

- When subtracting a positive integer, think of number line jumps.

- When subtracting a negative integer, use the shortcut where the double negative becomes a positive, and the subtraction turns into an addition.

Example 4. $-4 - 11$	**Example 5.** $4 - 11$
Think of a number line jump: you are at -4 and jump 11 steps to the left. You end up at -15.	Think of a number line jump: you are at 4 and jump 11 steps to the left. You end up at -7.

Example 6. $-4 - (-11)$	**Example 7.** $4 - (-11)$
Turn the double negative into a positive: $-4 - (-11) = -4 + 11$. Now think of the counters or a number line jump. The answer is 7.	Turn the double negative into a positive: $4 - (-11) = 4 + 11 = 15$.

2. Subtraction skills check-up! Subtract.

a. $(-4) - 6 =$ _____	**b.** $-3 - 7 =$ _____	**c.** $8 - (-9) =$ _____
$4 - (-6) =$ _____	$-3 - (-7) =$ _____	$(-8) - (-9) =$ _____

3. Find the missing integer.

a. $-4 +$ _____ $= -10$	**b.** $6 +$ _____ $= 0$	**c.** $5 -$ _____ $= -2$
$4 +$ _____ $= -2$	$-6 -$ _____ $= -4$	$4 +$ _____ $= 1$

4. Write an addition or subtraction sentence to match the number line jumps.

a. You are at ⁻6. You jump 5 to the right. You end up at _____.

b. You are at ⁻2. You jump 7 to the right. You end up at _____.

c. You are at 4. You jump 3 to the left. You end up at _____.

d. You are at 0. You jump 12 to the left. You end up at _____.

e. You are at 7. You jump 22 to the left. You end up at _____.

f. You are at ⁻7. You jump 22 to the right. You end up at _____.

5. Write an addition or subtraction sentence with integers to match these situations.

Situation	Addition or Subtraction Sentence
A miner was in an underground elevator, 65 m below the surface. The elevator descended 35 m. Now it is at an elevation of _____ m.	
Henry paid $150 for car repairs using a credit card (in other words, he made a debt). He paid $60 of the debt. Then he used the credit card again for another $120 of expenses. Now Henry owes $_____ on his credit card.	
Amy owed $180. She paid $40 of her debt. Her money situation is now _____.	
The temperature was 2°C. During the night it dropped 5 degrees. At dawn, it rose 2 degrees. Now the temperature is _____°C.	

6. Here is a funny riddle. Solve the math problems to uncover the answer.

L ____ $+ (-8) = -12$

O $3 + (-11) =$ ____

C $-2 -$ ____ $= -5$

S $-2 - (-4) =$ _____

S $-2 -$ _____ $= 5$

R $-24 - (-25) =$ _____

A ____ $+ 4 = 2$

I ____ $+ (-7) = 0$

O $-3 + 5 + (-5) =$ _____

A $7 -$ _____ $= -1$

M $(-144) + 150 =$ _____

H $77 - 90 =$ ____

I $-4 + (-15)$ _____

C $-7 +$ ____ $= 2$

What game do cows play at parties?

6	−8	−3	2	−19	9	8	−4		3	−13	−2	7	1	−7

Graphing

Remember? When an equation has two variables, there are many values of x and y that make that equation true.

Example. Note the equation $y = 2 - x$. If $x = 0$, then we can <u>calculate</u> the value of y using the equation: $y = 2 - 0 = 2$.

So, when $x = 0$ and $y = 2$, that equation is true. We can plot the number pair (0, 2) on the coordinate grid.

Some of the other (x, y) values that make the equation true are listed below, and they are plotted on the right.

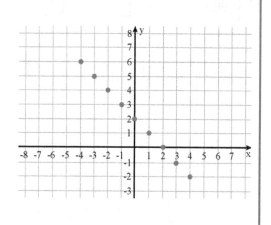

x	−4	−3	−2	−1	0	1	2	3	4
y	6	5	4	3	2	1	0	−1	−2

1. Plot the points from the equations. Graph both (b) and (c) in the same grid.

a. $y = x + 4$

x	−9	−8	−7	−6	−5	−4	−3	−2
y								

x	−1	0	1	2	3	4	5	6
y								

b. $y = 6 - x$

x	−3	−2	−1	0	1	2	3
y							

x	4	5	6	7	8	9
y						

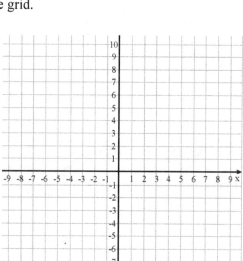

c. $y = x - 2$

x	−5	−4	−3	−2	−1	0	1	2
y								

x	3	4	5	6	7	8	9
y							

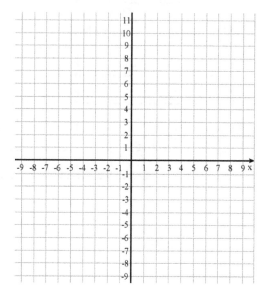

91

2. Continue the patterns according to the given rules, and then plot the points using the number pairs.

a.

add 1	x	−5	−4	−3	−2	−1
add 2	y	−8	−6	−4		

add 1	x	0	1	2	3	4
add 2	y					

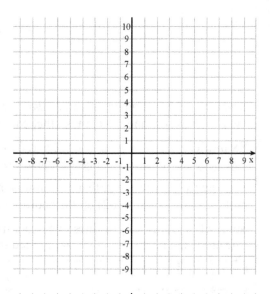

b.

add 2	x	−8	−6	−4		
subtract 3	y	9	6			

add 2	x					
subtract 3	y					

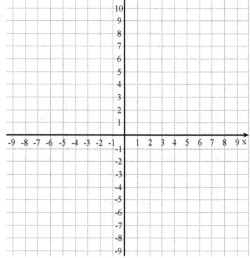

c. Make up your own rules.

	x					
	y					

	x					
	y					

Make another if you would like!

	x					
	y					

	x					
	y					

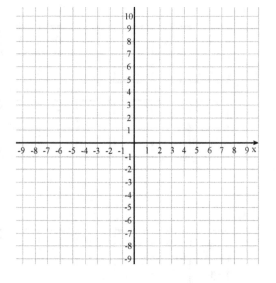

3. On March 1st, Natalie decided she would start to pay off her debt of $200. She decided she would pay $15 each week. Let t denote the number of weeks since March 1st. We can write in a table Natalie's progress with the payments. The variable a denotes her balance.

a. Fill in the table.

t	0	1	2	3	4	5	6	7	8	9	10	11	12	13
a	−200	−185	−170	−155										

b. Plot these points on the coordinate grid below.

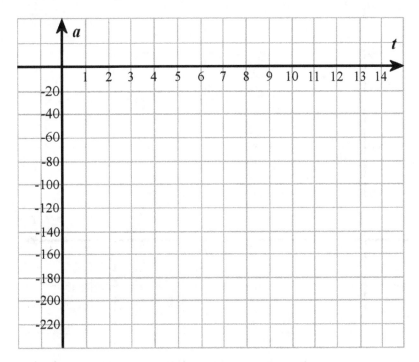

c. When will Natalie finish paying off her debt?

d. How can you see that from the graph?

4. **a.** Write the points from the graph in the table.

x								
y								

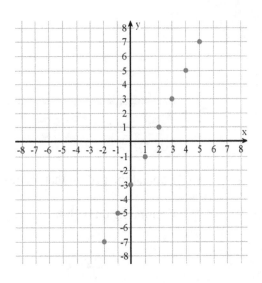

b. Find the pattern the x- and y-coordinates follow in (a), and use that same pattern to fill in the table below.

x	−8	−7	−6	−5	−4	−3	−2
y							−7

93

5. Sofia has $500 in her bank account on January 1st. Out of her bank account comes an automatic payment of $35, once a month, for Internet service. Let's say Sofia does not use this bank account for anything else. Let t be the number of months since January (January would be month zero).

   a. Fill in the table for Sofia's balance.

months	t	0	1	2	3	4	5	6	7	8	9	10	11	12
balance	a	$500												

   b. Plot the points.

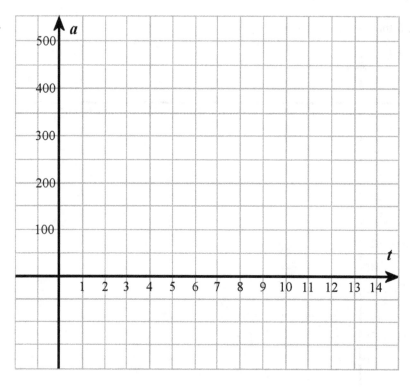

   c. If Sofia does not add more funds to her account, when will the account be negative?

   d. Let's say Sofia *forgets* to add more funds to her bank account. What is her balance at 14 months?

Puzzle Corner

x	0	1	2	3	4
y	6	4	2	0	−2

Look at the pattern that relates x and y.

Continuing on with the same pattern, what would y be when x is 100?

Mixed Review

1. Write an equation for each situation EVEN IF you could easily solve the problem without an equation! Then solve the equation.

   a. Katie is 54 years old. Shelly is 12 years younger than Katie. How old is Shelly?

   b. Bob bought some tulips for his wife. One tulip cost $2.15 The total cost was $45.15. How many tulips did Bob buy?

2. Find a number between 500 and 520 whose prime factorization has only 2s.

3. Write either a multiplication or a division, and solve.

a. How many times does ▭ go into ▭ ?	**b.** How many times does ◔ go into ✳ ?
c. Find $\dfrac{3}{4}$ of ◓	**d.** Find $\dfrac{2}{9}$ of ⊕

4. A package of cheap dominoes weighs 3 oz. A package of quality dominoes weighs 1 lb.

   a. How much does a box containing 50 packages of the cheap dominoes weigh? Give your answer in pounds and ounces.

   b. Another box contains 24 packages of the quality dominoes. Find how much more the box with quality dominoes weighs than the box with cheap dominoes.

5. Divide.

a. $2\frac{7}{8} \div \frac{2}{5}$	**b.** $4 \div 1\frac{5}{6}$
c. $5 \div \frac{2}{7}$	**d.** $10\frac{1}{10} \div \frac{3}{4}$

6. Annabelle can type 70 words in two minutes.
   How many words can she type in 15 minutes?

7. Mom and Dad's ages are in the ratio of 7:8.
   Dad is six years older than Mom. How old is Mom?

8. A rectangle's aspect ratio is 5:2, and
   its perimeter is 84 cm. Find its area.

9. Keith paid $414 of his salary in taxes. After that, he had $1,459 left.
   What percentage of his income did Keith pay in taxes?

10. Express these rates in the lowest terms.

a. 720 km : 4 hr	**b.** 6 kg for $4.20	**b.** 120 miles on 5 gallons

11. Simplify before you multiply.

a. $\frac{5}{36} \times \frac{24}{45}$	**b.** $\frac{16}{30} \times \frac{25}{24}$	**c.** $\frac{14}{25} \times \frac{35}{42}$

Integers Review

1. Compare. Write **<** or **>** in the box.

a. -1 ☐ -7	b. 2 ☐ -2	c. -6 ☐ 0	d. 8 ☐ -3	e. -8 ☐ -3

2. Order the numbers from the least to the greatest.

a. -6 2 -2 0	b. -14 -8 -11 -7

3. Express the situations using integers. Then compare them writing **>** or **<** in the box.

a. Lillian owes $12 and Hayley owes $18.	_____ ☐ _____
b. At 2 PM, the temperature was 5°C below zero. Now it is 2°C.	_____ ☐ _____
c. Joe rose in an elevator to the height of 16 m, whereas Gabriel went down 6 m below the ground.	_____ ☐ _____

4. Simplify. In (e), write using a number.

  a. $|-11|$ **b.** $|2|$ **c.** $|0|$ **d.** $-(-19)$ **e.** the opposite of 7

5. Draw a number line jump for each addition or subtraction sentence.

  a. $-9 + 6 =$ _____   **b.** $-2 + 5 =$ _____

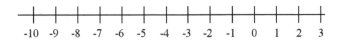

  c. $-3 - 5 =$ _____   **d.** $2 - 8 =$ _____

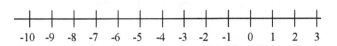

6. Write an addition or subtraction sentence.

  a. You are at ⁻10. You jump 6 to the right. You end up at _____.

  b. You are at ⁻5. You jump 8 to the right. You end up at _____.

  c. You are at 3. You jump 7 to the left. You end up at _____.

  d. You are at ⁻11. You jump 3 to the left. You end up at _____.

7. Add or subtract.

a.	b.	c.	d.
$2 + (-8) =$ _____	$-2 + (-9) =$ _____	$1 + (-7) =$ _____	$5 - (-2) =$ _____
$(-2) + 8 =$ _____	$2 - 8 =$ _____	$-4 - 5 =$ _____	$-3 - (-4) =$ _____

8. Write an addition or a subtraction sentence to match the situations.

   a. May has $35. She wants to purchase a guitar for $85.
   That would make her money situation be _____.

   b. A fish was swimming at the depth of 6 ft. Then he sank 2 ft.
   Then he sank 4 ft more. Now he is at the depth of _____ ft.

   c. Elijah owed his dad $20. Then he borrowed another $10.
   Now his balance is _____.

   d. The temperature was −13°C and then it rose 5°.
   Now the temperature is _____ °C.

9. Use mathematical symbols to express these ideas.

   a. the distance of −17 from zero   **b.** the opposite of −11

10. Which expression below matches with the situation? Jacob owes more than fifty dollars.

   a. balance $> -\$50$ **b.** balance $= -\$50$ **c.** balance $< \$50$ **d.** balance $< -\$50$

11. Plot the points from the function $y = 4 - x$
    for the values of x listed in the table.

x	−5	−4	−3	−2	−1	0	1	2
y								

x	3	4	5	6	7	8	9
y							

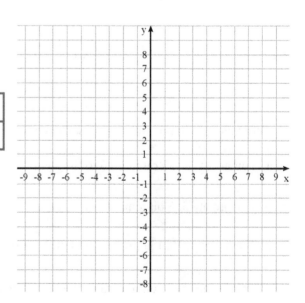

12. Find the missing integers.

a. $-2 + \underline{\hspace{1.5cm}} = -8$	**b.** $4 + \underline{\hspace{1.5cm}} = 0$	**c.** $5 - \underline{\hspace{1.5cm}} = -2$
$3 + \underline{\hspace{1cm}} = -2$	$-6 - \underline{\hspace{1.5cm}} = -12$	$3 + \underline{\hspace{1.5cm}} = 1$

13. Andrew drew a polygon, and then he reflected it
in the x-axis. The vertices of the reflected polygon
are: (−9, 6), (−6, 6), (−9, 3), and (−3, 0).
What were the coordinates of the original vertices?

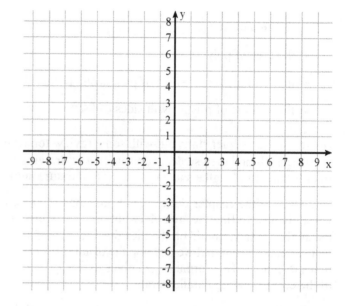

14. Find the distance between the points.

   a. (−3, −12) and (−3, 15)

   b. (−15, 34) and (−21, 34)

15. **a.** The points (−7, −3), (−1, −7), (−1, −1),
   and (−4, −6) are vertices of a quadrilateral.
   Draw the quadrilateral.

   b. Reflect the quadrilateral in the y-axis. (Draw
   the new quadrilateral). Write the coordinates
   of the moved vertices.

   (−7, −3) → (_____ , _____)

   (−1, −7) → (_____ , _____)

   (−1, −1) → (_____ , _____)

   (−4, −6) → (_____ , _____)

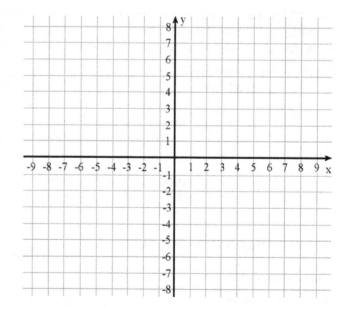

   c. Now move the already reflected quadrilateral 7 units up. (Draw the
   new quadrilateral). Write the coordinates of the new vertices.

   (_____ , _____)   (_____ , _____)   (_____ , _____)   (_____ , _____)

Chapter 9: Geometry
Introduction

The focus topics of this chapter are:

- the area of triangles

- the area of polygons

- nets and the surface area of prisms and pyramids

- the volume of prisms with sides of fractional length

However, the chapter starts out with some review topics from earlier grades. We review the different types of quadrilaterals and then students do some basic drawing exercises. In these drawing problems, students will need a ruler to measure lengths and a protractor to measure angles.

One focus of the chapter is the area of polygons. To reach this goal, we follow a step-by-step development. First, we study how to find the area of a right triangle, which is very easy, as a right triangle is always half of a rectangle. Next, we build on the idea that the area of a parallelogram is the same as the area of the related rectangle, and from that we develop the usual formula for the area of a parallelogram as the product of its base times its height. This formula then gives us a way to generalize finding the area of any triangle as *half* of the area of the corresponding parallelogram.

Finally, the area of a polygon can be determined by dividing it into triangles and rectangles, finding the areas of those, and summing them up. Students also practice their new skills in the context of a coordinate grid. They draw polygons in the coordinate plane and find the lengths of their sides, perimeters, and areas.

Nets and surface area is another major topic. Students draw nets and determine the surface area of prisms and pyramids using nets. They also learn how to convert between different area units, not using conversion factors or formulas, but using logical reasoning where they learn to determine those conversion factors themselves.

Lastly, we study the volume of rectangular prisms, this time with edges of fractional length. (Students have already studied this topic in fifth grade for prisms with edges that are a whole number long.) The basic idea is to prove that the volume of a rectangular prism *can* be calculated by multiplying its edge lengths even when the edges have fractional lengths. To that end, students need to think how many little cubes with edges ½ or ⅓ unit go into a larger prism. Once we have established the formula for volume, students solve some problems concerning the volume of rectangular prisms.

There are quite a few videos available to match the lessons in this chapter at https://www.mathmammoth.com/videos/ (choose 6th grade).

The Lessons in Chapter 9

Helpful Resources on the Internet

QUADRILATERALS REVIEW AND DRAWING

Classifying Quadrilaterals Review
Test your knowledge of quadrilaterals with this multiple-choice quiz.
http://www.thegreatmartinicompany.com/geometry/classifying-quadrilaterals-triangles.html

Quadrilateral Types
Identify quadrilaterals based on pictures or attributes in this interactive online quiz.
https://www.khanacademy.org/math/geometry/hs-geo-foundations/hs-geo-polygons/e/quadrilateral_types

Quadrilateral Problems in the Co-ordinate Grid
Try these five problems involving quadrilaterals on the co-ordinate plane.
https://www.khanacademy.org/math/6th-engage-ny/engage-6th-module-5/6th-module-5-topic-b/a/rectangles-on-the-coordinate-plane-examples

Drawing Triangles
Drag the vertices of the triangle to construct a new triangle that has the given angle measures.
https://khanacademy.org/math/in-seventh-grade-math/seventh-practical-geometry/new-topic-2015-11-17T01:34:20.426Z/e/constructing-triangles

AREA

Area of a Parallelogram
Explore the area of parallelograms with this activity that goes through step-by-step and shows you how to come up with a formula (in words or algebra) to calculate the area of any parallelogram.
http://www.interactive-maths.com/area-of-a-parallelogram-ggb.html

Area of Parallelograms Quiz
Practice finding the area of parallelograms in this interactive online quiz.
http://www.xpmath.com/forums/arcade.php?do=play&gameid=11

Area of Triangles
This article explains why the area of a triangle is half of base times height. Practice problems are included.
https://www.khanacademy.org/math/cc-sixth-grade-math/cc-6th-geometry-topic/cc-6th-area-triangle/a/area-of-triangle

Triangle Explorer
Practice calculating the area of a triangle using this interactive tool.
http://www.shodor.org/interactivate/activities/TriangleExplorer/

Area of Polygons by Drawing
Explore polygons and their areas with this interactive online tool.
http://www.mathsisfun.com/geometry/area-polygon-drawing.html

Area Tool
Use this tool to determine how the base and the height of a figure can be used to determine its area. Can you find the similarities and differences between the area formulas for trapezoids, parallelograms, and triangles?
http://illuminations.nctm.org/Activity.aspx?id=3567

Area of Shapes on a Grid
Practice finding the areas of triangles and quadrilaterals on grids in this interactive online exercise.
https://www.khanacademy.org/math/cc-sixth-grade-math/cc-6th-geometry-topic/cc-6th-area-shapes-grid/e/area-of-triangles-2

Area of Irregular Shapes
Find the area of various irregular shapes in this interactive online activity.
https://www.studyladder.com/games/activity/area-of-irregular-shapes-13136

Free worksheets for the area of triangles, quadrilaterals, and polygons
Generate printable worksheets for finding the area of triangles, parallelograms, trapezoids, or polygons in the coordinate grid. Options include scaling, image size, workspace, border, and more.
http://www.homeschoolmath.net/worksheets/area_triangles_polygons.php

BBC Bitesize - Area
Brief revision (review) "bites," including a few interactive questions, about the area of triangles, parallelograms, and compound shapes.
http://www.bbc.co.uk/bitesize/ks3/maths/measures/area/revision/4/

VOLUME & SURFACE AREA

Solid Shapes and Their Nets
Read about simple solid shapes, click to rotate them, and practice finding their nets.
http://gwydir.demon.co.uk/jo/solid/index.htm

Geometric Solids
Manipulate (rotate) various geometric solids by dragging with the mouse and see their nets.
http://illuminations.nctm.org/Activity.aspx?id=3521

Explore and Play with Prisms
Use the animation at the bottom of the page to explore the properties of four prisms. You can highlight the numbers of faces (F), vertices (V), and edges (E) for each prism.
http://www.learner.org/interactives/geometry/3d_prisms.html

Explore and Play with Pyramids
Use the animation at the bottom of the page to explore the properties of four pyramids. You can highlight the numbers of faces (F), vertices (V), and edges (E) for each prism.
http://www.learner.org/interactives/geometry/3d_pyramids.html

Interactive Solids
Visualize and rotate the following solids: cube, cuboids (a.k.a rectangular prism), tetrahedron, square pyramid, octahedron, triangular prism, and cylinder. Click the button "unfold" to see the net of each solid.
https://www.homeschoolmath.net/interactives/3D_shapes.php

Nets of Polyhedra
Practice matching 2D nets to the 3D shapes that they fold up into in this interactive activity.
https://www.khanacademy.org/math/geometry/hs-geo-foundations/hs-geo-area/e/nets-of-3d-figures

Interactivate: Surface Area and Volume
Explore or calculate the surface area and volume of rectangular prisms and triangular prisms. You can change the base, height, and depth interactively.
http://www.shodor.org/interactivate/activities/SurfaceAreaAndVolume

Making Cuboids
An interactive activity to explore the surface area and volume of cuboids, calculate them, or find the volume when the areas of the faces are known.
https://www.mrbartonmaths.com/resources/keystage3/shape/Volume%20and%20Surface%2

Surface Area of a Rectangular Prism
Practice calculating the surface area of a rectangular prism with this interactive animation.
https://www.learner.org/interactives/geometry/area_surface.html

Surface Area
Practice finding the area of 3D objects in this interactive online activity.
https://www.khanacademy.org/math/in-fifth-grade-math/boxes-sketching/representing-3d-objects-nets/e/surface-areas

Worksheets for the Volume and Surface Area of Rectangular Prisms
Customizable worksheets for volume/surface area of cubes and rectangular prisms. Includes the option of using fractional edge lengths.
http://www.homeschoolmath.net/worksheets/volume_surface_area.php

Volume with Fractions
Practice finding the volume of rectangular prisms that have fractional side lengths in this interactive exercise.
https://www.khanacademy.org/math/basic-geo/basic-geo-volume-sa/volume-with-fractions/e/volume_with_fractions

Volume Problems with Fractions
Solve volume problems involving objects like fish tanks, truck beds, and refrigerators in this online exercise.
https://www.khanacademy.org/math/basic-geo/basic-geo-volume-sa/volume-with-fractions/e/volume-word-problems-with-fractions

Exploring Surface Area, Nets, and Volume
This interactive resource allows the user to explore the concepts of surface area, volume, 3D shapes, and nets. Shapes include rectangular and triangular prisms; rectangular and triangular pyramids; cylinders; and cones. The resource includes print activities, solutions, and learning strategies.
http://learnalberta.ca/content/mejhm/?
l=0&ID1=AB.MATH.JR.SHAP&ID2=AB.MATH.JR.SHAP.SURF&lesson=html/object_interactives/surfaceArea/use_it.html

JUST FOR FUN

Online Kaleidoscope
Create your own kaleidoscope pattern with this interactive tool.
http://www.zefrank.com/dtoy_vs_byokal/

Interactivate! Tessellate
Choose a shape, then edit its corners or edges. The program automatically changes the shape so that it will tessellate (tile) the plane. Then push the tessellate button to see your creation!
http://www.shodor.org/interactivate/activities/Tessellate

Quadrilaterals Review

The chart shows the seven different types of quadrilaterals as a "family," descending from the generic quadrilateral at the top.

If a quadrilateral is listed under another, it means the two have like a "parent-child" relationship: the quadrilateral listed lower (the child) has its parent's characteristics.

Number in the chart the following types of quadrilaterals:

1. rhombus   5. scalene quadrilateral

2. kite   6. trapezoid

3. rectangle   7. parallelogram

4. square

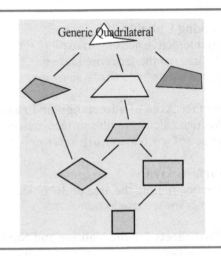

Generic Quadrilateral

1. Find the correct type of quadrilateral for each definition.

   a. A quadrilateral with four congruent sides.

   b. A quadrilateral where the opposite sides are parallel.

   c. A quadrilateral with one pair of parallel sides.

   d. A quadrilateral with two pairs of congruent sides, where each pair of congruent sides are touching.

   e. A quadrilateral with four congruent sides and four right angles.

2. Think of the "parent-child" relationships as shown in the chart, and answer the questions:

   a. Is a rhombus also a kite?

   b. Is a rectangle also a parallelogram?

   c. Is a trapezoid also a rectangle?

3. Reflect the parallelograms in the coordinate grid.

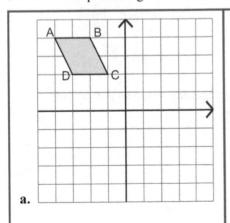

a.

Reflect the parallelogram
in the *x*-axis.

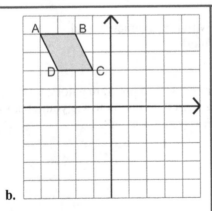

b.

Reflect the parallelogram
in the *y*-axis.

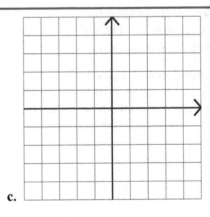

c.

Draw your own parallelogram.
Then reflect it both in the *x*-axis
and in the *y*-axis.

4. Draw a trapezoid where the parallel
   sides measure 4 cm and 7 cm.
   Use the proper tools (a ruler in this case).
   Is there only one such trapezoid,
   or could there be several different ones?

5. Draw a rhombus with 6 cm sides
   and with 30° and 150° angles.
   (Hint: Start with the 30° angle. Then mark off
   the 6-cm sides. Next, draw the 150° angle.)

Drawing Problems

In each problem:

- First, try to visualize the figure.

- Next, decide which part you should draw first: a given side, or a given angle. Sometimes it is possible to draw the figure starting either way.

1. Draw a parallelogram with a 10-cm side, a 6-cm side, and a 60° angle between those sides.
   Hint: The four angles of a parallelogram add up to 360°, so the other angle you need is 120°.

These two pictures illustrate how it is ENOUGH to know the measurements of two angles and the length of the side *between* them in order to draw a triangle.

In other words, you do not have to know *all* the angles and the sides in order to draw a triangle —just two angles and a side is sufficient.

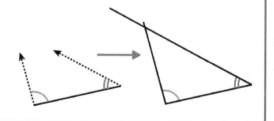

2. Draw a triangle that has a 25° angle, a 115° angle, and a 3″ side between those angles.

3. **a.** Draw an isosceles triangle
with a 78° top angle and
two 7.6-cm sides.
Hint: start out by drawing the top angle.

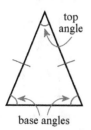

b. Measure the base angles of your
triangle. They should be congruent;
however, it is very hard to draw
so accurately that you would get
the same angle measurements for
the base angles, so don't worry if
they differ a little.

4. **a.** Draw an isosceles triangle with
a 4″ base and 35° base angles.

b. What is the measurement of the top angle?

c. How long are the other two sides?

5. Draw a copy of this triangle. Your triangle should match
this triangle exactly if they were placed on top of each other.

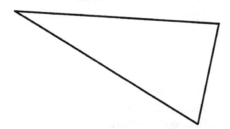

Area of Right Triangles

This rectangle is divided into two right triangles that are **congruent.** This means that if you could flip one of them and move it on top of the other, they would match exactly.

The rectangle has an area of 2 × 4 = 8 square units.
Can you figure out what the area of just *one* of the triangles is?

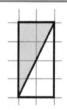

Here the area of the whole rectangle is 3 × 5 = 15 square units.
How could you figure out the area of just one of the triangles?

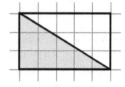

Here the sides of the triangle are 6 and 3 units. The other two sides of the rectangle are drawn with dotted lines. The area of the *rectangle* is 18 square units. The area of just the triangle is half of that, or 9 square units.

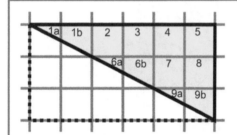

Let's look closer at the last triangle above. To confirm that its area is 9 square units, we can *count* the little squares in the triangle.

Notice that some of the parts do not cover a complete square, but by combining those we can make whole squares and then count them.

1. Find the area of these right triangles. To help you, trace the "helping rectangle" for the triangles.

a. _____ square units

b. _____ square units

c. _____ square units

d. _____ square units

e. _____ square units

f. _____ square units

g. _____ square units

h. _____ square units

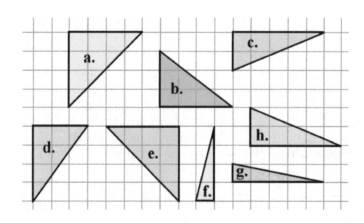

To find the area of a right triangle, **multiply the lengths of the two sides** that are perpendicular to each other (in other words, the two that form the right angle). Then **take half of that.**

This works because the area of the right triangle is exactly _____ of the area of the rectangle.

108

2. Draw a right triangle whose two perpendicular sides are given below, and then find its area.

   a. 1.2 cm and 5 cm

   b. 2 1/2 inches and 1 1/4 inches

We can find the area of this house-shape in three parts.

1. The square has an area of 4 × 4 = 16 square units.

2. Triangle 2 has perpendicular sides of 3 and 2 units,
   so its area is (1/2) × 2 × 3 = 3 square units.

3. Triangle 3 is the same shape and size as triangle 2,
   so its area is also 3 square units.

Lastly, add the areas: 16 + 3 + 3 = 22 square units in total.

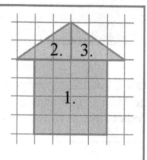

---

3. Find the areas of these compound shapes.

a. 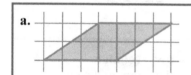   **b.** 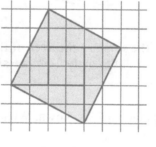   **c.**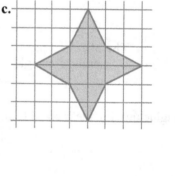

4. Draw a right triangle whose *area* is 13 square centimeters.
   Can you only draw one right triangle with that area, or several different kinds?
   Explain.

5. In the grid, draw 3 different right triangles that each have an area of 6 square units.

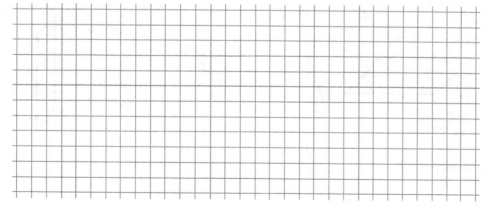

Area of Parallelograms

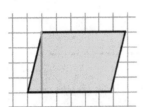 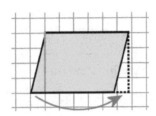 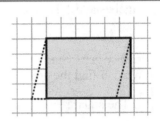

We draw a line from one vertex of the parallelogram in order to form a *right triangle*. Then we move the triangle to the other side, as shown. Look! We get a *rectangle*!

The rectangle's area is 6 × 4 = 24 square units, and that is *also the area of the original parallelogram.*

It works here, as well. The area of the rectangle and of the parallelogram are the same: both have the area of 4 × 4 = 16 square units.

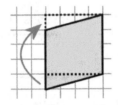 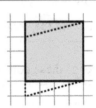

The area of a parallelogram is the same as the area of the corresponding rectangle.
You construct the rectangle by moving a right triangle from one side of the parallelogram to the other.

1. Imagine moving the marked triangle to the other side as shown. What is the area of the original parallelogram?

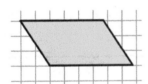 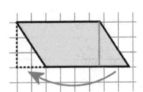

2. Draw a line in each parallelogram to form a right triangle. Imagine moving that triangle to the other side so that you get a rectangle, like in the examples above. Find the area of the rectangle, thereby finding the area of the original parallelogram.

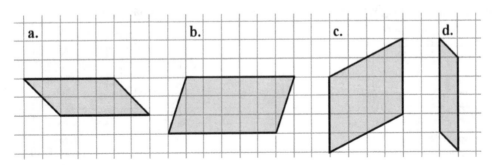

a. _____ sq. units   **b.** _____ sq. units   **c.** _____ sq. units   **d.** _____ sq. units

110

One side of the parallelogram is called the **base**. You can choose any of the four sides to be the base, but people often use the "bottom" side.

A line segment that is *perpendicular* to the base and goes from the base to the opposite side of the parallelogram is called the **altitude**.

When we do the trick of "moving the triangle," we get a rectangle. One of its sides is congruent (has the same length) to the parallelogram's *altitude*. The other side is congruent to the parallelogram's *base*.

That is why you can simply multiply **BASE × ALTITUDE** to get the area of a parallelogram.

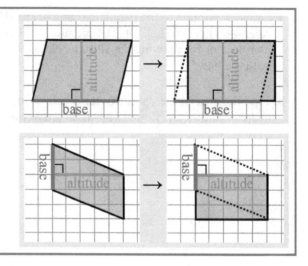

3. Draw an altitude to each parallelogram. Highlight or "thicken" the base. Then find the areas.

   a. _____ sq. units

   b. _____ sq. units

   c. _____ sq. units

   d. _____ sq. units

   e. _____ sq. units

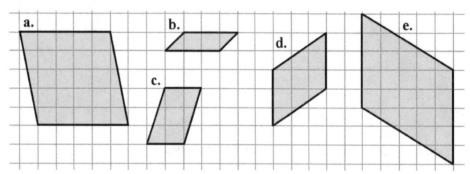

4. **a.** Draw the altitudes to the parallelograms and mark their bases. The altitude of one parallelogram is already marked. Notice how that altitude does not "reach" the base, but instead ends at the continuation of the base. That is no problem—what matters is that the altitude is *perpendicular* to the base.

   b. Find the areas of these parallelograms. What do you notice?

5. Draw as many differently-shaped parallelograms as you can that all have an area of 12 square units.

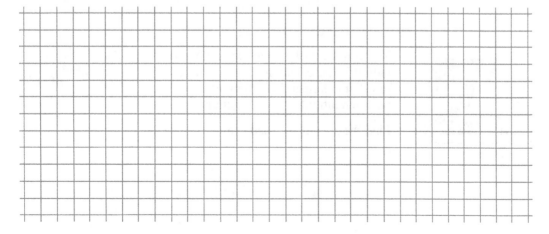

6. **a.** Draw an altitude to the parallelograms below. Use a protractor or a triangular ruler—do not "eyeball" it. The picture on the right shows how to position a protractor for drawing the altitude. Notice that the 90° mark is aligned with the base.

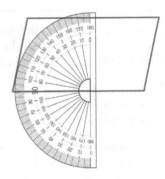

b. Find the area of the parallelograms below, measuring the necessary parts to the nearest millimeter. Round your final answer to whole square centimeters.

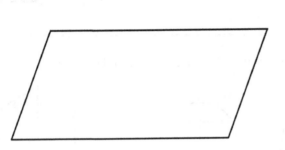

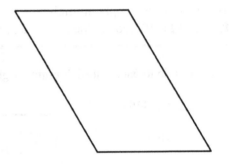

7. Find the area of the parallelogram in square inches.

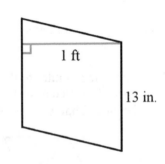

1 ft

13 in.

8. Find the area of the parallelogram in square meters.

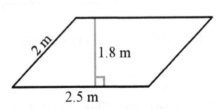

2 m

1.8 m

2.5 m

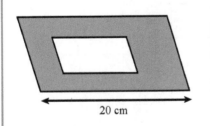

20 cm

The altitude of the larger parallelogram is half of its base, and the base and altitude of the smaller parallelogram are half the base and altitude of the larger one.

Find the area of the shaded area.

Puzzle Corner

Area of Triangles

We can always put any triangle together with a copy of itself to make a parallelogram.

Therefore, **the area of the triangle must be exactly half of the area of that parallelogram.**

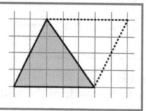

1. Find the area of the shaded triangle in the picture above.

2. Draw the corresponding parallelograms for these triangles, and find their areas.
   Hint: Draw a line that is congruent to the base of the triangle, starting at the top vertex.

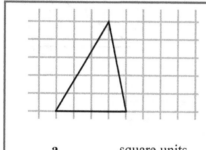   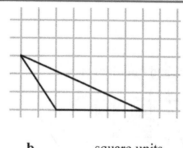   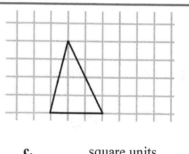

a. _____ square units   **b.** _____ square units   **c.** _____ square units

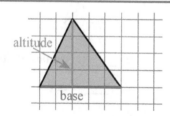

Again, we use a base and an altitude. The **base** can be any side of the triangle, though people often use the "bottom" side.

The **altitude** is *perpendicular* to the base, and it goes from the opposite vertex to the base (or to the continuation of the base).

Since the area of a triangle is *half* of the area of the corresponding parallelogram, we can calculate the area as *half* of the base times the altitude, or:

$$AREA = \frac{BASE \times ALTITUDE}{2}$$

You can choose any side to be the base. Here, it makes sense to choose the vertical side as the base.

The area is $\frac{4 \times 6}{2} = 12$ square units.

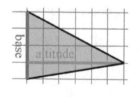

3. Draw an altitude in each triangle, and mark the base. Find the area of each triangle.

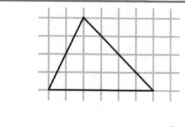   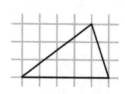   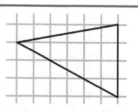

a. _____ square units   **b.** _____ square units   **c.** _____ square units

Example 1. The altitude of a triangle may fall *outside* of the triangle itself. It is still perpendicular to the base, and starts at a vertex.

The corresponding parallelogram is seen if you follow the dotted lines.

The area is $\dfrac{3 \times 3}{2}$ = 4 ½ square units.

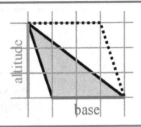

Example 2. Here it is easiest to think of the base being on the top. Again, the altitude falls outside of the actual triangle.

The area is $\dfrac{5 \times 3}{2}$ = 7 ½ square units.

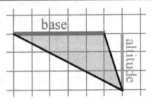

4. Draw the base and the altitude to this triangle, and find its area.

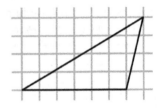

5. Draw altitudes and bases in the triangles, and find their areas.

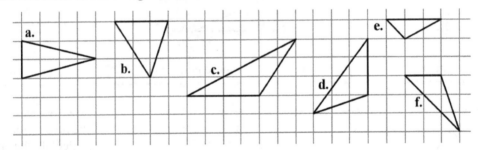

a. _____ square units   **b.** _____ square units   **c.** _____ square units

d. _____ square units   **e.** _____ square units   **f.** _____ square units

6. This figure is called a _____.

   Calculate its area.

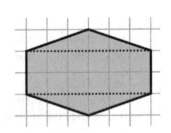

7. Draw as many different-shaped triangles as you can that have an area of 12 square units.

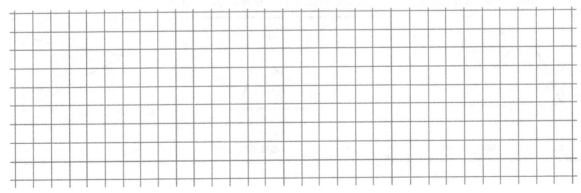

How to find the area of a triangle not drawn on a grid

1. First, choose one of the sides as the base. It can be any side!

2. Draw the altitude. Use a protractor or a triangular ruler to draw the altitude so that it goes through one vertex and is perpendicular to the base. See the illustration.

   Line up the 90°-mark on the protractor with the base of the triangle and slide it until the line you draw will pass through the vertex.

3. Measure the lengths of the altitude and base as precisely as you can with a ruler.

4. Calculate the area.

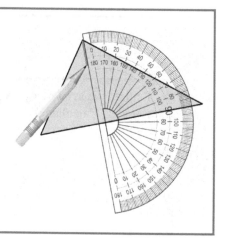

8. Find the area of this triangle in square centimeters. Round your final answer to the nearest whole square centimeter. (You will need to draw an altitude in the triangle.)

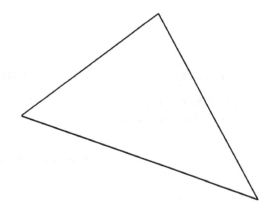

9. Find the area of this triangle in square inches.

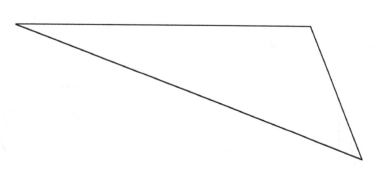

10. Draw your own triangle, and find its area!

11. Draw a triangle with an *area* of 3 square inches. Is it only possible to draw just *one* triangle with that area, or is it possible to draw several different ones, with varying shapes/sizes?

Draw a triangle, *without measuring anything,* so that its area is close to 20 cm². Check by drawing the altitude and measuring! Practice until you get a triangle with an area of approximately 20 cm². You can even make a game out of this.

Puzzle Corner

Area of Polygons

To calculate the **area of a polygon**, all you have to do is divide it into easy shapes, such as rectangles and triangles. Calculate the area of each easy shape separately, and add them to find the total area.

1. This figure is called a _____.

   Calculate its area using the three triangles.
   For each triangle, use the *vertical* side as the base.

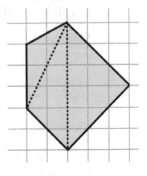

2. Here is another way of calculating the area of the same figure.

   1. Calculate the area of the rectangle that encloses the figure.
   2. Calculate the areas of the four shaded triangles.
   3. Subtract.

   Use this method and verify that you get the same result as above.

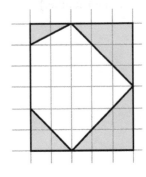

3. Find the areas of the shaded figures.

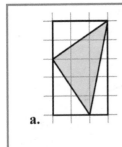

a.

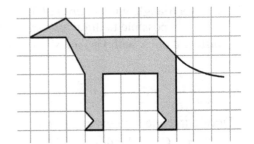

b.

4. **a.** The side of each little square in the drawing on the right is 1 inch. Find the area of the polygon.

   b. Imagine that the side of each little square is 2 inches instead. What is the area now?

116

5. Calculate the total area of the figures.

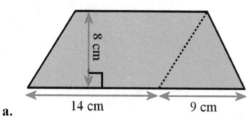

a.

8 cm

14 cm   9 cm

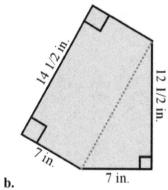

b.

14 1/2 in.

12 1/2 in.

7 in.

7 in.

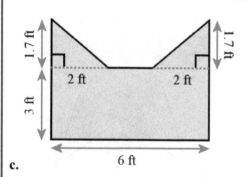

c.

1.7 ft

1.7 ft

2 ft   2 ft

3 ft

6 ft

6. Divide this quadrilateral into two triangles, and then find its area in square centimeters. You may use a calculator.

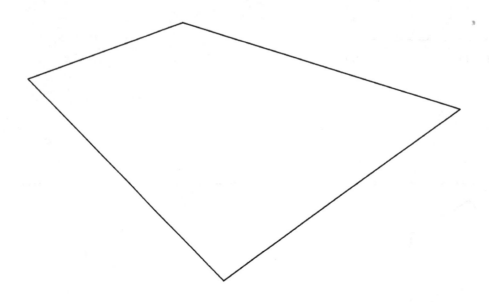

Puzzle Corner

Measure what you need to from this star to find: (a) its perimeter in centimeters and (b) its area in square centimeters.

Polygons in the Coordinate Grid

Here is a neat way to **find the area of any polygon whose vertices are points in the grid.**

(1) Draw a rectangle around the polygon.
(2) Divide the area between the polygon and the rectangle into triangles and rectangles.
(3) Calculate those areas.
(4) <u>Subtract</u> the calculated areas from the total area of the large rectangle to find the area of the polygon.

Example. To find the area of the colored triangle, we draw a rectangle around it that is 3 units by 6 units. Then we find the areas marked with 1, 2, 3, 4, and 5:

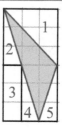

1: a triangle; $3 \times 3 \div 2 = 4.5$ square units
2: a triangle; $1 \times 3 \div 2 = 1.5$ square units
3: a rectangle; $1 \times 3 = 3$ square units
4: a triangle; $1 \times 3 \div 2 = 1.5$ square units
5: a triangle; $1 \times 3 \div 2 = 1.5$ square units
The total for the shapes 1, 2, 3, 4, and 5 is 12 square units.

Therefore, the area of the colored triangle is 18 square units − 12 square units = 6 square units.

1. Use the method above to find the area of these triangles with given vertices.

   a. (−8, 7), (−5, 3), and (4, 0).

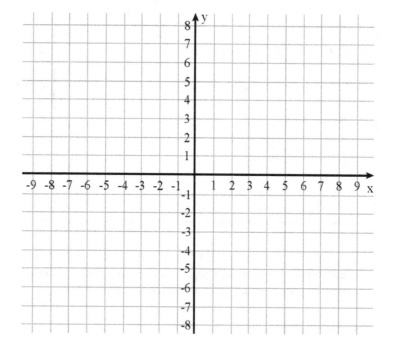

   b. (−7, −2), (−2, −1), and (−4, −7).

2. Draw a quadrilateral in the grid with vertices
(8, 5), (3, 4), (4, −5), (7, −6)

Use the same technique to find its area.

3. Draw any pentagon using grid points as vertices. Then find its area.

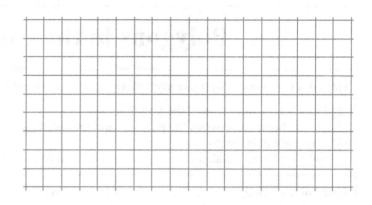

4. Name the polygons, transform them, and find their area.

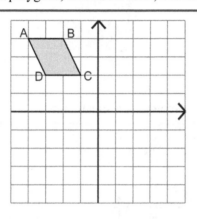

a. What is this polygon called?

b. Reflect it in the *x*-axis.

c. Find its area.

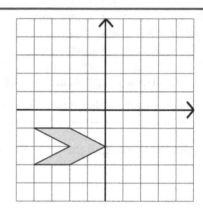

d. What is this polygon called?

e. Move it 4 units up, and 2 units to the right.

f. Find its area.

5. The points (1, 2.4), (2.4, 1), (2.4, −1), (1, −2.4) are four vertices of a water fountain in the shape of a regular octagon. The other four points are found by reflecting these four in the *y*-axis.

   a. Draw the octagon.

   b. Find the length of *one* side of the fountain.

   c. Find its perimeter.

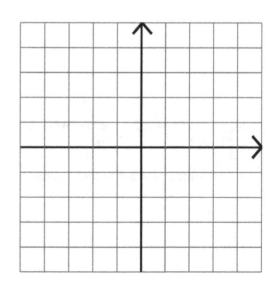

6. A hotel wants to build a swimming pool with a total area between 100 and 140 square meters. One of its sides has to be 12.5 meters.

   a. Suggest three different rectangular shapes and draw them in the grids below. Each unit in the grid is 5 m.

   b. For each pool, calculate its area.

   c. For each pool, give the distance from the driveway to the edge of the pool.

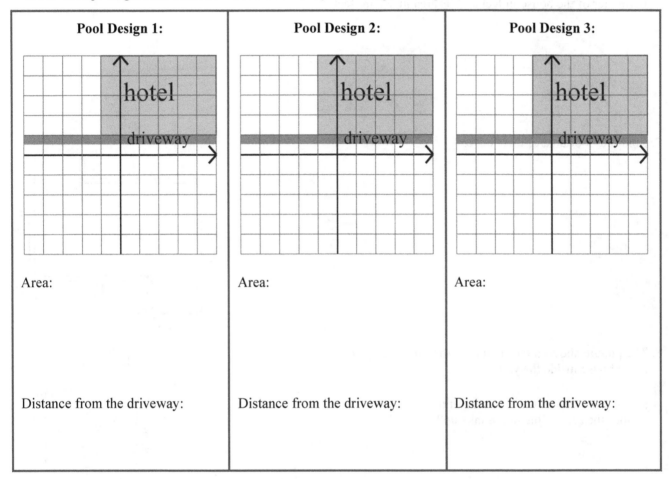

Pool Design 1:	Pool Design 2:	Pool Design 3:
Area:	Area:	Area:
Distance from the driveway:	Distance from the driveway:	Distance from the driveway:

Puzzle Corner Join the following points in order with line segments, and then find the area of the resulting polygon.

(−35, −40), (−35, 40), (−20, 40), (20, −15), (20, 40), (35, 40), (35, −40), (20, −40), (−20, 15), (−20, −40) and (−35, −40)

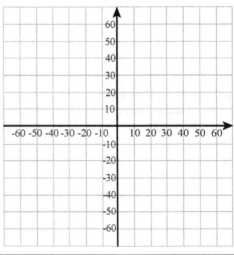

121

Area and Perimeter Problems

1. On paper, Mr. Smith's house plan measures 9″ × 12″.
   In reality, the house is 40 times as big. Find the
   perimeter of the house in feet and its area in square feet.

2. Find the floor area of this house.

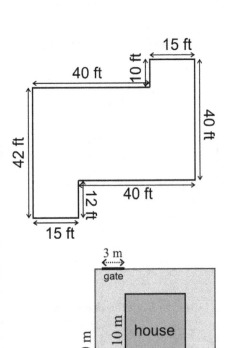

3. The picture shows a rectangular yard with a 3 m gate,
   and a house inside the yard.

   a. What fraction of the total area of the yard
   does the area of the house take up?

   b. Find the area of the actual yard, not including
   the area that the house takes up.

   c. Find the cost of fencing this yard
   when the fence costs $11.59 per meter,
   and the gate costs $120.

4. A father is leaving a plot of land to his two children. In his will, he specifies it to be divided into two parts as shown. The two children are not sure which part is bigger.

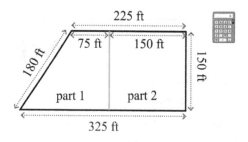

a. Find the area of part 2.

b. Find the area of part 1.

c. Find the area of the whole plot.

d. How many percent is the area of part 1 of the total area?

e. How many percent is the area of part 2 of the total area?

f. If the whole plot is valued at $45,000, find the value of part 1 and part 2 to the nearest dollar.

5. These are designs for a decorative tiling. What fractional part of each design consists of the darker color?

a.

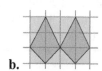

b.

6. This is a front side of a house. Find its area. The dimensions are given in feet.

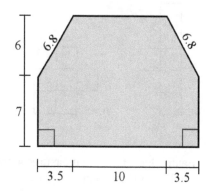

123

Nets and Surface Area 1

Review: Solids

This pyramid is a **solid** or a three-dimensional figure. Other solids you are familiar with are the cube, the cone, the rectangular prism, and the sphere (ball). They are called three-dimensional figures because they are not flat objects on paper but reside in space, in three dimensions.

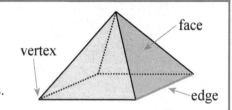

A **face** of a solid is a flat "side" that has an area.
An **edge** is the line segment where two faces meet.
A **vertex** is a corner where three or more edges meet.

This picture shows a flat figure, called a **net**, that can be folded up to form a solid, in this case a cube.

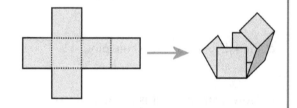

Each face of a cube is a square. If we find the total area of its faces, we will have found the **surface area** of the cube.

Let's say that each edge of this cube measures 2 cm. Then one face would have an area of 2 cm × 2 cm = 4 cm^2, and the total surface area of the six faces of the cube would be 6 × 4 cm^2 = 24 cm^2.

What is its volume? Remember, **volume** has to do with how much space a figure takes up, and not with "flat" area. Volume is measured in *cubic* units, whereas area is measured in *square* units. The volume of this cube is 2 cm × 2 cm × 2 cm = 8 cm^3.

This is the net of the pyramid above (not drawn to the same scale, but smaller). Imagine folding it into a pyramid.

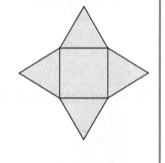

We can see its bottom face is a square, and the other faces are triangles.

To find its surface area, we would simply find the area of the bottom square and the area of the triangles, and add those.

Imagine filling a pyramid with tiny little cubes and then counting how many there are. That's its volume. You'll learn a simple formula for the volume of a pyramid in a higher grade. (Or you can look it up now on the Internet or in an encyclopedia!)

1. Which of these patterns are nets of a cube? Which ones can be folded into a cube?
   You can check your answers by copying the patterns on paper, cutting them out, and folding them.

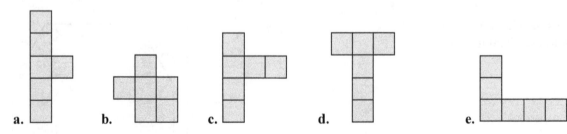

  a.   b.   c.   d.   e.   f.

2. Each edge of a cube measures 4 cm.
   Find its surface area.

3. Match each rectangular prism (a), (b), (c), and (d) with the correct net (1), (2), (3), and (4).
   Again, if you would like, you can copy the nets onto paper, cut them out, and fold them.

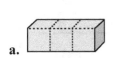 a.   b.   c. 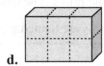 d.

(1) (2) (3) (4)

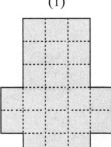  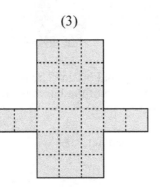 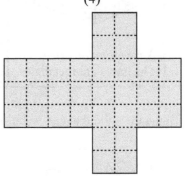

4. Find the surface area, A, and volume, V, of each rectangular prism above if the edges of the little cubes are
   1 cm long.

a. A = _____ cm^2 **b.** A = _____ cm^2 **c.** A = _____ cm^2 **d.** A = _____ cm^2

V = _____ cm^3 V = _____ cm^3 V = _____ cm^3 V = _____ cm^3

5. Find the surface area, A, and volume, V, of each rectangular prism above if the edges of the little cubes are
   2 cm long.

a. A = _____ cm^2 **b.** A = _____ cm^2 **c.** A = _____ cm^2 **d.** A = _____ cm^2

V = _____ cm^3 V = _____ cm^3 V = _____ cm^3 V = _____ cm^3

6. The surface area of a cube is 96 square inches.

   a. What is the area of one face of the cube?

   b. How long is each edge of the cube?

   c. Find the volume of the cube.

7. The *volume* of a cube is 27 cubic feet.
   Find its surface area.

Prisms

A prism has two identical polygons as its top and bottom faces. These polygons are called the *bases* of the prism. The bases are connected with faces that are parallelograms (and often rectangles).

Prisms are named after the polygon used as the bases.

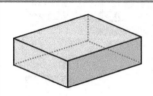		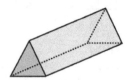
A *rectangular prism*. The bases are rectangles.	A hexagonal prism. The bases are hexagons. Notice, one of the bases is facing you.	A triangular prism. Again, the base is facing you.

8. Name the solid that can be built from each net.

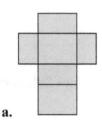

a.

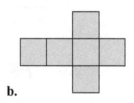

b.

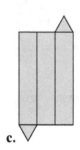

c.

9. Name the solids that can be built from these nets, and calculate their surface area.

a. solid: _____

surface area: _____

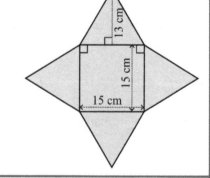

b. solid: _____

surface area: _____

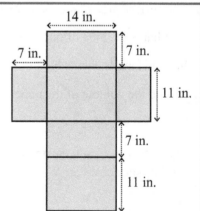

126

Nets and Surface Area 2

1. Draw a net for each of these rectangular prisms.

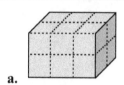

a.

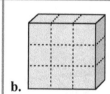

b.

2. Which expression, (1), (2), or (3), can be used to calculate the surface area
   of this prism correctly? (You do not have to calculate the surface area.)

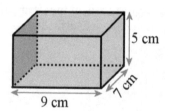

5 cm

7 cm

9 cm

1. 2×35 cm^2 + 2×63 cm^2 + 2×45 cm^2

2. 5 cm $\times$ 9 cm $\times$ 7 cm

3. 5 cm $\times$ 7 cm + 9 cm $\times$ 7 cm + 9 cm $\times$ 5 cm

3. Ryan organized the calculation of the surface area of this prism into three parts. Complete the calculations.

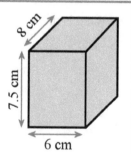

8 cm

7.5 cm

6 cm

Top and bottom:

Back and front:

The two sides:

Total:

4. This box for chocolate is in the shape of a triangular prism.

    a. Draw a net for the prism.

    b. Calculate its surface area.

5. A gift box is in the shape of a cube with 20-cm sides.
   Calculate its surface area.

6. Annie wants to cover the sides of this box with one long piece of pretty
   wrapping paper. She does NOT want to cover the bottom or the top.

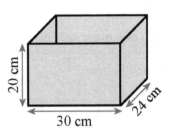

    a. What is the length and width of the piece of wrapping paper she needs?

    b. What is the area of the wrapping paper?

7. Draw a net for each solid, and then calculate the surface area.

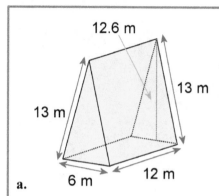

a.

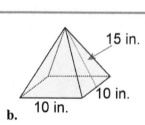

b.

8. A swimming pool is in the shape of a rectangular prism.
   It is 12.5 m long, 6 m wide, and 2 m deep.

   a. Sketch the swimming pool and mark the dimensions on the sketch.

   b. In order to tile the pool, find the surface area of the pool's
   bottom and sides (not including the top, since it won't be tiled).

   c. Tile costs $9.90 per square meter.
   Calculate the cost of tiling the pool.

Converting Between Area Units

I could tell you conversion factors for different units of area, such as 1 square mile = 27,878,400 square feet, but instead I want to show you *how YOU can figure them out yourself!* It is actually pretty simple!

The side of each *little* square is 1 inch. Therefore, the side of the *big* square is 12 inches, or 1 foot. This means the big square has an area of 1 square foot.

So, how many *square inches* are there in one square foot?

1 sq. ft = 12 in × 12 in

= _____ sq. in.

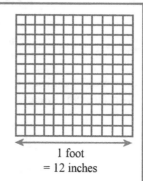

1 foot
= 12 inches

The image shows 1 square centimeter. It is divided into square millimeters. The side of the whole square is 1 cm and at the same time 10 mm.

How many square millimeters are in one square centimeter?

$1 \text{ cm}^2 = 10 \text{ mm} \times 10 \text{ mm}$

= _____ mm^2

1. The sides of the large square measure 1 yard. How many square feet are there in 1 square yard?

   1 sq. yd. = _____ ft × _____ ft = _____ sq. ft.

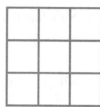

2. Sketch a square with 1-meter sides. Each side is _____ cm.

   The area in square *meters* is ____ m × _____ m = _____ m^2.

   The area in square *centimeters* is _____ cm × _____ cm = _____ cm^2.

3. Imagine or sketch a square with 2-meter sides.

   The area in square *meters* is ____ m × _____ m = _____ m^2.

   The area in square *centimeters* is _____ cm × _____ cm = _____ cm^2.

4. Imagine or sketch a rectangle with 3 ft and 8 ft sides.

   The area in square *feet* is ____ ft × _____ ft = _____ ft^2.

   The area in square *inches* is _____ in × _____ in = _____ in^2.

5. Use similar reasoning to determine:

   a. How many square yards are in one square mile?

    | 1 mi = 1,760 yd

   b. How many square meters are in one square kilometer?

6. Measure what you need from the figures and find their areas in square millimeters and in square centimeters.

a. _____ mm^2 **b.** _____ mm^2 **c.** _____ mm^2

_____ cm^2 _____ cm^2 _____ cm^2

7. Think of the relationship between square centimeters and square millimeters, for example, based on the previous exercise. How can you convert 58 square centimeters into square millimeters?

8. **a.** Find the area of a 0.8 mi. by 2 mi. rectangle in square miles.

| 1 mi = 5,280 ft |

   b. Now find the same area in square feet.

9. A village lies within a rectangle that has 0.2 km and 0.15 km sides.
   Find its area in square *meters*.

10. Connect the dots in the figure below to get a quadrilateral, or draw your own non-rectangular quadrilateral on blank paper.

   a. Draw and measure what you need, and find the area of the quadrilateral in <u>square millimeters</u>.
   Round it to the nearest hundred.

   b. Find the area to the nearest <u>square centimeter</u>.

Volume of a Rectangular Prism with Sides of Fractional Length

Example 1. The edges of this little cube each measure 1/2 cm. If we stack eight of them so that we get a bigger cube... we get this:	The bigger cube has <u>1 cm edges, so its volume is 1 cubic centimeter.</u> If eight identical little cubes make up this bigger cube, and its volume is 1 cubic centimeter, then <u>the volume of *one* little cube is 1/8 cubic centimeter.</u> Notice: this is the same result that we get if we multiply the height, width, and depth of the little cube: $$\frac{1}{2}\,\text{cm} \times \frac{1}{2}\,\text{cm} \times \frac{1}{2}\,\text{cm} = \frac{1}{8}\,\text{cm}^3$$

1. The edges of each little cube measure 1/2 cm. What is the total volume, in cubic centimeters, of these figures?

a.	**b.**	**c.** 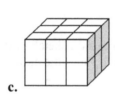	**d.** 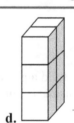
width = __*1/2*__ cm	width = _____ cm	width = _____ cm	width = _____ cm
height = _____ cm	height = _____ cm	height = _____ cm	height = _____ cm
depth = _____ cm	depth = _____ cm	depth = _____ cm	depth = _____ cm
__*1*__ little cube, 1/8 cm^3	__*8*__ little cubes, each 1/8 cm^3	_____ little cubes, each 1/8 cm^3	_____ little cubes, each 1/8 cm^3
V = __*1/8*__ cm^3	V = _____ cm^3	V = _____ cm^3	V = _____ cm^3

2. Write a *multiplication* to calculate the volume of the figures (c) and (d) above, and verify that you get the same result as above.

a. V = _____ cm × _____ cm × _____ cm =	**b.** V = _____ cm × _____ cm × _____ cm =

3. Fill in.

This time, the edges of each little cube measure 1/3 inch.

(Mark the dimensions on the little cube.)

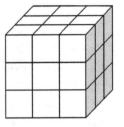

We put _____ of the little cubes together to form one cubic inch (on the right). →

Since the big cube measures 1 cubic inch, and there are _____ little cubes,

the volume of each little cube is _____ cubic units. This is the same answer that we find

by multiplying: V = _____ in × _____ in × _____ in = _____ in³.

4. Show that the volume of a box that measures 1 1/3 in. by 2 in. by 2/3 in. is indeed

$$V = \frac{4}{3} \text{ in} \times 2 \text{ in} \times \frac{2}{3} \text{ in} = \frac{16}{9} \text{ in}^3.$$

How?

   (i) Build a physical model or draw a sketch of the box,
        using 1/3 in. by 1/3 in. by 1/3 in. little cubes.

   (ii) Count the number of little cubes needed.

   (iii) Multiply the number of little cubes by the volume of ONE little cube.

5. Show that the volume of a box with dimensions of 3/4 in. by 2 1/4 in. by 1 in. is indeed

$$V = \frac{3}{4} \text{ in} \times \frac{9}{4} \text{ in} \times 1 \text{ in} = \frac{27}{16} \text{ in}^3.$$

How?

   (i) Build a physical model or draw a sketch of the box,
        using 1/4 in. by 1/4 in. by 1/4 in. little cubes.

   (ii) Count the number of little cubes needed.

   (iii) Multiply the number of little cubes by the volume of ONE little cube.

6. The edges of each little cube measure <u>1/3 in</u>. What is the total volume of these figures, in cubic units?

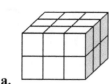

a.

width = <u>1</u> in

height = <u>2/3</u> in

depth = _____ in

_____ little cubes,
each 1/27 in^3

V = _____

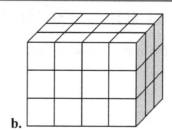

b.

width = _____ in

height = _____ in

depth = _____ in

_____ little cubes,
each 1/27 in^3

V = _____

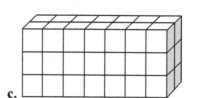

c.

width = _____ in

height = _____ in

depth = _____ in

_____ little cubes,
each 1/27 in^3

V = _____

You have already learned that the **volume of a rectangular prism** can be calculated by multiplying the width, depth, and height. As a formula: $V = w \times d \times h$ or just V = *wdh*.

This formula also applies when the dimensions are fractions or decimals.

Example 2. Calculate the volume of this box.

We simply multiply the three dimensions, using mixed numbers:

$\frac{7}{3}$ ft $\times \frac{3}{2}$ ft $\times 1$ ft $= \frac{7}{2}$ ft^3 = 3 ½ ft^3.

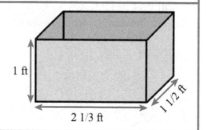

1 ft

2 1/3 ft

1 1/2 ft

7. Write a multiplication to calculate the volume of the figures in exercise 6, and verify you get the same result.

a. V = _____ in × _____ in × _____ in =

b. V = _____ in × _____ in × _____ in =

c. V = _____ in × _____ in × _____ in =

Volume Problems

1. **a.** Calculate the volume of this carton to the nearest cubic centimeter.

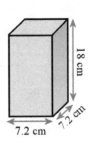

   b. Considering that 1 milliliter = 1 cubic centimeter, what is the volume of the carton in milliliters?

   c. The carton is filled 96% full with juice. How many milliliters of juice does it contain?

2. Mike drew a model for a box on the computer.

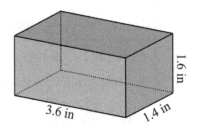

   a. The real box is 10 times as large as the model. Calculate the dimensions, in inches and in feet, of the real box.

   b. Calculate the volume, in cubic feet, of the real box.

3. Each edge of a "magic" cube toy measures 2¼ inches.

   a. Calculate its volume.

   b. How many of these cubes could you pack into a box
   that measures 2 ft by 1 ft by 1 ft?
   Hint: Draw a sketch, and think in inches, not feet.

 You work for a store that sells aquariums. Fill in the chart below.
Round the volume in liters to the <u>nearest liter</u>.
Round the volume in gallons to the <u>nearest 1/4 gallon</u>.

<u>Note 1:</u> There are many ways to figure out the volume in gallons and liters. You can use some of these conversion factors (you will not need them all):

1 milliliter = 1 cubic centimeter	1 cubic inch = 0.554113 fluid ounces
1 gallon = 4 quarts = 128 fluid ounces	1 cubic inch = 16.387064 cubic centimeters

<u>Note 2:</u> The dimensions in centimeters have been rounded. For example, 10 inches is not exactly 25 ½ cm.

STANDARD TANKS			
DIMENSIONS	**VOLUME**	**DIMENSIONS**	**VOLUME**
Inches	**Gallons**	**Centimeters**	**Liters**
16 × 8 × 10		41 × 20¼ × 25½	
20 × 10 × 12		51 × 25 × 30	
24 × 12 × 16		61 × 30½ × 40½	
36 × 12 × 17		91½ × 30½ × 43	
36 × 18 × 16		92½ × 46 × 41	
36 × 18 × 18		92½ × 46 × 46	

Mixed Review

1. A family put 1/3 of 60 pounds of flour into the cellar.
   Then, they gave 3/8 of the remaining flour to a neighbor.
   How much flour did the neighbor get?

2. Multiply.

a. $3 \times 0.3 \times 0.08 =$ _____	**b.** $7 \times 0.2 \times 1.1 =$ _____	**c.** $0.25 \times 10^5 =$ _____
d. $0.0009 \times 8 =$ _____	**e.** $0.002 \times 100 =$ _____	**f.** $3000 \times 0.0007 =$ _____

3. Order the fractions from the smallest to the biggest.

a. $\dfrac{5}{6}, \dfrac{8}{10}, \dfrac{7}{8}, \dfrac{9}{10}, \dfrac{7}{10}$	**b.** $\dfrac{9}{8}, \dfrac{11}{10}, \dfrac{7}{6}, \dfrac{12}{10}, \dfrac{10}{8}$
___ < ___ < ___ < ___ < ___	___ < ___ < ___ < ___ < ___

4. Convert the measurements into the given units.

   a. 0.9 L = _____ dl = _____ cl = _____ ml

   b. 2,800 m = _____ km = _____ dm = _____ cm

   c. 56 g = _____ dg = _____ cg = _____ mg

5. Convert. Round your answers to 2 decimals in (a) - (d). In (e) and (f) use whole numbers.

a. 76 oz = _____ lb	**c.** 3.6 gal = _____ qt	**e.** 2.67 mi = _____ ft
b. 98 in = _____ ft	**d.** 0.483 lb = _____ oz	**f.** 5.09 ft = _____ ft _____ in

6. Use ratios to convert the measuring units. 1 kg = 2.2 lb, and 1 in = 2.54 cm.

a. 134 kg into pounds
b. 156 in. into centimeters

7. Solve the equations.

a. $0.2m = 6$	**b.** $0.3p = 0.09$	**c.** $y - 1.077 = 0.08$

8. **a.** Draw a picture where there are 2 triangles for each 5 squares, and a total of 21 shapes.

   b. The unit rates are:

   _____ squares for **1** triangle

   _____ triangles for **1** square

9. Add and subtract.

a. $5 + (-8) =$ _____	**b.** $-11 + (-9) =$ _____	**c.** $2 + (-17) =$ _____	**d.** $2 - (-8) =$ _____
$(-5) + 8 =$ _____	$9 - 11 =$ _____	$-3 - 8 =$ _____	$-8 - (-2) =$ _____

10. A figure whose vertices are at $(-5, -3)$, $(-1, -3)$, $(0, -5)$, and $(-7, -5)$ is transformed this way:

   1. It is reflected in the x-axis.
   2. It is moved four units to the right, five down.
   3. It is reflected in the y-axis.

   Give the coordinates of its vertices after all three transformations.

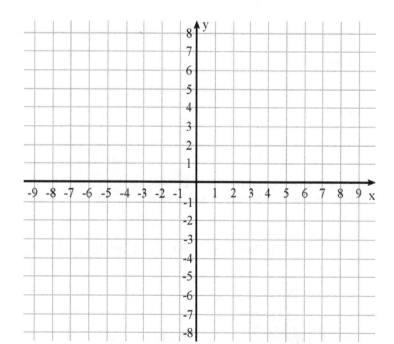

11. Draw a triangle whose vertices are at $(-3, -4)$, $(5, -4)$, and $(2, 7)$.

   Draw an altitude to the triangle.

   Find its area.

12. A mole is digging a tunnel at the speed of 4 m per hour.

   a. Choose a letter variable to represent the time the mole
   has dug and another to represent the length (distance)
   of tunnel it has dug.

   b. Fill in the table. Plot the points.

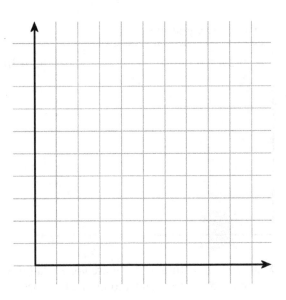

time (hours)	0	1	2	3	4	5	6	7	8	9
distance (meters)										

   c. Write an equation relating the two variables.

   d. Which is the independent variable?

13. Fill in the blank and give an example.

   a. Dividing a number by 5 is the same as multiplying it by _____. Example:

   b. Dividing a number by $\frac{2}{3}$ is the same as multiplying it by _____. Example:

14. Write as percentages. If necessary, round your answers to the nearest percent.

   a. 5/8

   b. 6/25

15. Draw a triangle with 55° and 29° angles,
    and a 6-cm side between those angles.

16. Draw a rhombus with 7.5 cm sides, and one 66° angle.

Puzzle Corner   Find the missing factors.

a. $\frac{1}{5} \times \underline{\quad} = \frac{1}{20}$ **b.** $\frac{1}{5} \times \underline{\quad} = 2$ **c.** $\frac{5}{6} \times \underline{\quad} = \frac{1}{3}$

Geometry Review

1. Explain how the area of the triangle is related to the area of the parallelogram.

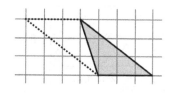

2. Find the area of the quadrilaterals in square units.

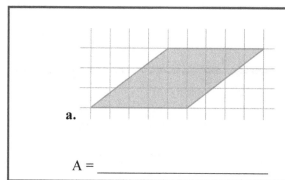

a.

A = _____

b.

A = _____

3. **a.** Jeremy planted a garden in the shape of the diagram at the right. Find the area of Jeremy's garden.

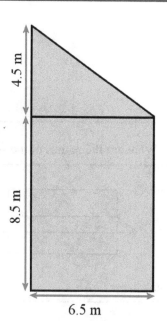

4.5 m

8.5 m

6.5 m

   b. Jeremy planted a rectangular section measuring 3.5 m by 3 m with green beans. What percentage of his garden did he plant with green beans?

4. Find the area of this triangle:

   a. in square centimeters

   b. in square millimeters

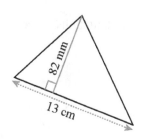

82 mm

13 cm

5. Draw a net and calculate the surface area

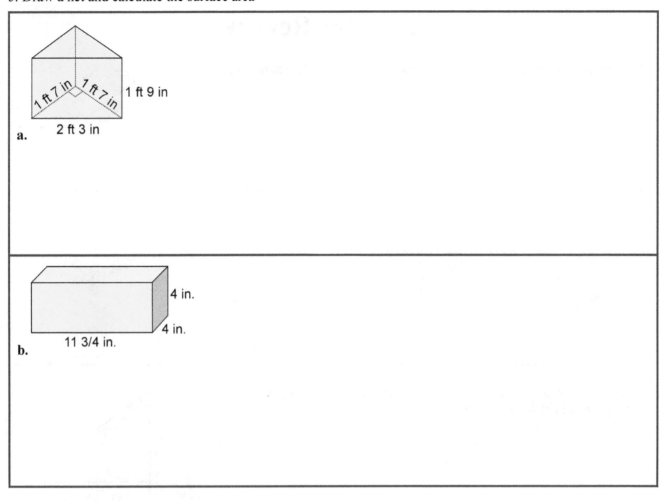

a.

b.

6. What are the names of the solids that can be constructed from these nets?

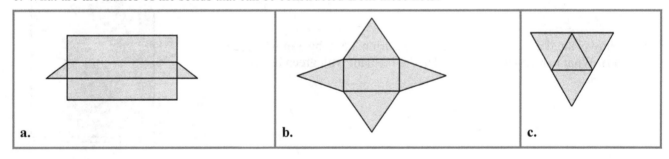

a.

b.

c.

7. What solid can you build from this net?

Calculate its surface area.

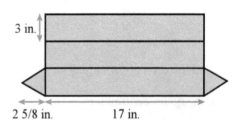

8. The edges of each little cube measure 1/3 m.

   What is the total volume, in cubic centimeters, of the figure at the right?

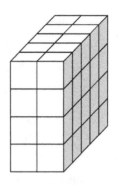

9. This building has three stories. Calculate the volume of *one* story.

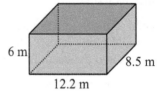

6 m   8.5 m   12.2 m

10. An aquarium measures 50 cm × 30 cm on the bottom, and its height is 40 cm.
    It is 4/5 filled with water.

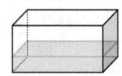

   How many cubic centimeters of water is in it?

   How many milliliters of water is in it?
   (One cubic centimeter is one milliliter.)

   How many liters?

Chapter 10: Statistics
Introduction

The fundamental theme in our study of statistics is the concept of *distribution*. In the first lesson, students learn what a distribution is—basically, it is *how* the data is distributed. The distribution can be described by its center, spread, and overall shape. The shape is read from a graph, such as a dot plot or a bar graph.

Two major concepts when summarizing and analyzing distributions are its center and its variability. First we study the center, in the lessons about mean, median, and mode. Students not only learn to calculate these values, but also relate the choice of measures of center to the shape of the data distribution and the type of data.

In the lesson *Measures of Variation* we study range, interquartile range, and mean absolute deviation. The last one takes many calculations, and the lesson gives instructions on how to calculate it using a spreadsheet program, such as Excel.

Then in the next lessons, students learn to make several different kinds of graphs: histograms, boxplots, and stem-and-leaf plots. In those lessons, students continue summarizing distributions by giving their shape, a measure of center, and a measure of variability.

There are some videos available for these topics at https://www.mathmammoth.com/videos/ (choose 6th grade).

The Lessons in Chapter 10

Helpful Resources on the Internet

Statistical Questions
Practice spotting the difference between statistical and non-statistical questions in this interactive online exercise.
https://www.khanacademy.org/math/cc-sixth-grade-math/cc-6th-data-statistics/cc-6-statistical-questions/e/statistical-questions

Shape of Distributions
Practice explaining the shapes of data distributions in this interactive online activity.
https://www.khanacademy.org/math/probability/data-distributions-a1/displays-of-distributions/e/shape-of-distributions

MEASURES OF CENTRAL TENDENCY

Mean, Median, Mode, and Range
Lesson on how to calculate the mean, median, and mode for a set of data given in different ways.
It also has interactive exercises.
http://www.cimt.org.uk/projects/mepres/book8/bk8i5/bk8_5i2.htm

Measures of Center Quiz
Test your knowledge of mean, median, mode, and range with this interactive multiple-choice quiz.
http://www.phschool.com/webcodes10/index.cfm?wcprefix=ana&wcsuffix=8254

Central Measures
This page includes an illustrated lesson about how to find the central values. Scroll down to the bottom and click on the questions to practice the concept.
http://www.mathsisfun.com/data/central-measures.html

Mean and Median from Plots Quiz
Practice finding the mean and median by reading various types of plots in this 10-question online quiz.
https://www.thatquiz.org/tq-5/?-jr0t0-l2-nk-p0

Choosing the Best Measure of Center
Read the lesson and use the practice problems to help you learn how to choose the best measure of center.
https://www.khanacademy.org/math/probability/data-distributions-a1/summarizing-center-distributions/a/choosing-the-best-measure-of-center

How Mean and Median Are Affected When Adding a Data Point
Practice figuring out how the mean and median are affected when a data point is added to, taken from, or shifted within a data set.
https://www.khanacademy.org/math/probability/data-distributions-a1/summarizing-center-distributions/e/effects-of-shifting-adding-removing-data-point

Measures Activity
Enter your own data and the program will calculate mean, median, mode, range and some other statistical measures.
http://www.shodor.org/interactivate/activities/Measures

GCSE Bitesize Mean, Mode and Median Lessons
Tutorials with simple examples.
http://www.bbc.co.uk/schools/gcsebitesize/maths/statistics/measuresofaveragerev1.shtml

Math Goodies Interactive Statistics Lessons
Clear lessons with examples, interactive quiz questions, practice exercises, and challenge exercises over topics that include range, arithmetic mean, non-routine mean, median, and mode.
http://www.mathgoodies.com/lessons/toc_vol8.html

MEASURES OF VARIATION

Interquartile Range (IQR)
Practice finding the interquartile range of small sets of data.
https://www.khanacademy.org/math/probability/data-distributions-a1/summarizing-spread-distributions/e/calculating-the-interquartile-range--iqr-

Mean Deviation
A simple explanation about what the mean absolute deviation is, how to find it, and what it means.
http://www.mathsisfun.com/data/mean-deviation.html

Mean Absolute Deviation
Several videos explaining how to calculate the mean absolute deviation of a data set.
http://www.onlinemathlearning.com/measures-variability-7sp3.html

Working with the Mean Absolute Deviation (MAD)
A tutorial and questions where you are asked to create line plots with a specified mean absolute deviation.
http://www.learner.org/courses/learningmath/data/session5/part_e/working.html

Mean Deviation

This page contains an illustrated lesson on the mean deviation. Scroll down the page to find questions to practice the concept.

http://www.mathsisfun.com/data/mean-deviation.html

Calculate the Mean Absolute Deviation

Practice finding the mean absolute deviation (MAD) of a data set in this interactive online exercise.

https://www.khanacademy.org/math/cc-sixth-grade-math/cc-6th-data-statistics/cc-6-mad/e/calculating-the-mean-absolute-deviation--mad-

GRAPHING AND GRAPHS

Create a Histogram

Explore already-made histograms using given sets of data, or use your own data to make your own. Try changing the interval size (the bin size) to see how it affects the graph.

http://www.shodor.org/interactivate/activities/Histogram/

Make Your Own Histogram

To use this histogram, set your interval (this varies depending on the numerical values of your data), describe the x and y axes, and enter the numerical data. Lastly, click "create graph."

http://mrnussbaum.com/graph/histogram/

Boxplots Quiz

Practice reading boxplots in this 10-question online quiz.

https://www.thatquiz.org/tq-5/?-jo7t0-l3-p0

Understanding Quartiles

Practice understanding the meaning of quartiles of data sets in this interactive online activity.

https://www.khanacademy.org/math/probability/data-distributions-a1/box--whisker-plots-a1/e/interpreting-quartiles-on-box-plots

Make Your Own Boxplot

Enter values from your own data, and this web page creates your box-and-whisker plot for you.

http://www.mrnussbaum.com/graph/bw.htm

Create a Boxplot

You can explore boxplots using the given sets of data, or make your own. Try adding more data to the existing data sets and see how the plot changes.

http://www.shodor.org/interactivate/activities/BoxPlot/

Box-and-Whisker Plots Quiz

Review box-and-whisker plots with this interactive self-check quiz.

http://www.phschool.com/webcodes10/index.cfm?wcprefix=bja&wcsuffix=1203

Measures of Center and Quartiles Quiz from ThatQuiz.org

An online quiz about the measures of center and quartiles in boxplots, stem-and-leaf plots, and dot plots.

http://www.thatquiz.org/tq-5/?-jr0t0-l1-p0

Reading Stem-and-Leaf Plots

Read the stem-and-leaf plot and answer the question correctly.

https://www.khanacademy.org/math/pre-algebra/pre-algebra-math-reasoning/pre-algebra-stem-leaf/e/reading_stem_and_leaf_plots

Stem-and-Leaf Plots Quiz

Practice the mean and median in this 10-question online quiz involving stem-and-leaf plots.

https://www.thatquiz.org/tq-5/?-ji4t0-l2-p0

Make Your Own Stem-and-Leaf Plot

Enter values from your own data, and this web page creates your stem-and-leaf plot for you.

http://www.mrnussbaum.com/graph/sl.htm

Stem-and-Leaf Plots Quiz

An online multiple-choice quiz that is created randomly. Refresh the page (or press F5) to get another quiz.
http://www.phschool.com/webcodes10/index.cfm?wcprefix=asa&wcsuffix=0905&area=view

Graphs Quiz from ThatQuiz.org

This quiz asks questions about different kinds of graphs (bar, line, circle graph, multi-bar, stem-and-leaf, boxplot, scattergraph). You can modify the quiz parameters to your liking, such as to plot the graph, answer different kinds of questions about the graph, or find mean, median, or mode based on the graph.
http://www.thatquiz.org/tq-5/math/graphs

Create a Graph

Children can create bar graphs, line graphs, pie graphs, area graphs, and xyz graphs to view and print.
http://nces.ed.gov/nceskids/createagraph/default.aspx

Statistics Interactive Activities from Shodor

A set of interactive tools for exploring and creating different kinds of graphs and plots. You can enter your own data or explore the examples.

http://www.shodor.org/interactivate/activities/BarGraph/

http://www.shodor.org/interactivate/activities/Histogram/

http://www.shodor.org/interactivate/activities/CircleGraph/

http://www.shodor.org/interactivate/activities/MultiBarGraph/

http://www.shodor.org/interactivate/activities/PlopIt/

PlotLy

A comprehensive, collaborative data analysis and graphing tool. Bring data in from anywhere, do the math, graph it with interactive plots (scatter, line, area, bar, histogram, heatmap, box, and more), and export it.
http://plot.ly

Comparing Data Displays

Practice interpreting and comparing dot plots, histograms, and box plots in this interactive online exercise.
https://www.khanacademy.org/math/pre-algebra/pre-algebra-math-reasoning/pre-algebra-frequency-dot-plot/e/comparing-data-displays

Exploring Election Data

This interactive mathematics resource allows students to explore and interpret Alberta provincial election results from 1905 to 2004 using a pictograph, line graph, bar graph, circle graph, or data table. The resource includes print activities, solutions, and learning strategies.
http://learnalberta.ca/content/mejhm/?
I=0&ID1=AB.MATH.JR.STAT&ID2=AB.MATH.JR.STAT.DATA&lesson=html/object_interactives/Data_Display/use_it.html

FACTS & FIGURES

GapMinder

Visualizing human development trends (such as poverty, health, gaps, income on a global scale) via stunning, interactive statistical graphs. This is an interactive, dynamic tool and not just static graphs. Download the software or the reports for free.
http://www.gapminder.org/data/

WorldOdometers

World statistics updated in real time. Useful for general educational purposes - for some stunning facts.
http://www.worldometers.info

UN Data

The United Nations offers the ability to search across its statistical databases, including education, human development, population, trade, and more.
http://data.un.org

Understanding Distributions

A **statistical question** is a question where we expect a range of *variability* in the answers to the question.

For example, "How old am I?" is *not* a statistical question (there is only one answer), but "How old are the students in my school?" *is* a statistical question, because we expect the students' ages not to be all the same.

"How much does this TV cost?" is *not* a statistical question because we expect there to be just one answer.

"How much does this TV cost in various stores around town?" *is* a statistical question, because we expect a number of different answers: the prices in different stores will vary.

To answer a statistical question we collect a set of **data** (many answers). The data can be displayed in some kind of a graph, such as a bar graph, a histogram, or a dot plot.

This is a **dot plot** showing the ages of the participants in a website-building class. Each dot in the plot signifies one observation. For example, we can see there was one 13-year old and two 14-year olds in the class.

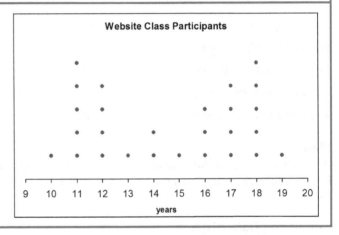

The dot plot shows us the **distribution** of the data: it shows how many times (the frequency) each particular value (age in this case) occurs in the data.

This distribution is actually **bimodal,** or "double-peaked." This means it has two "centers": one around 11-12 years, and another around 17-18 years.

1. Are these statistical questions? If not, change the question so that it becomes a statistical question.

   a. What color are my teacher's eyes?

   b. How much money do the students in this university spend for lunch?

   c. How much money do working adults in Romania earn?

   d. How many children in the United States use a cell phone regularly?

   e. What is the minimum wage in Ohio?

   f. How many sunny days were there in August, 2013, in London?

   g. How many pets does my friend have?

We are often interested in the **center**, **spread**, and **overall shape** of the distribution. Those three things can summarize for us what is important about the distribution.

The **center** of a distribution has to do with its peak.

These three dot plots show how the **spread** of a distribution can vary. This means how the items of data items are spread—whether they are "spread" all over, or tightly concentrated near some value, or somewhat concentrated around some value. We will study more about spread in another lesson.

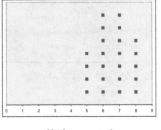

little spread

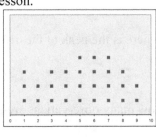

medium spread

large spread

The distribution can have many varying overall **shapes.** For example:

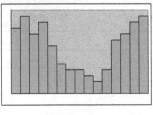

U-shaped

double-peaked (bimodal)

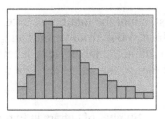

asymmetrical, right-tailed
(a.k.a. right-skewed)

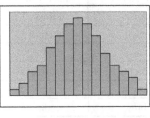

bell-shaped (normal)

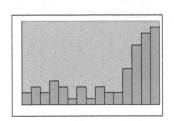

J-shaped

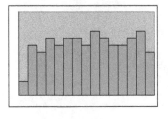

rectangular

2. Anne asked her classmates the question, "How tall are you?" The histogram shows the distribution of her data.

a. Describe the shape of the distribution.

b. Where is the peak of the distribution?

c. How many observations are there?

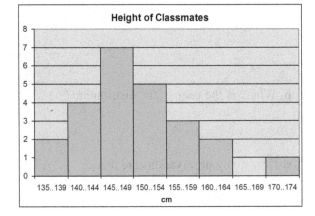

3. Make a dot plot from this data (weekly work hours of a restaurant's employees). You need to place a dot for each observation.

48 45 46 41 42 42 43 43 42 42 41
41 45 49 40 41 41 42 46 47 42 40

a. Describe the shape of the distribution.

b. Where is the peak of the distribution?

c. How many observations are there?

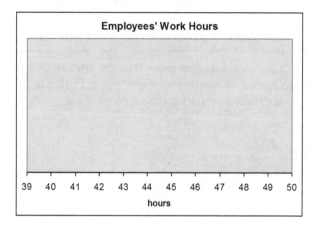

4. First, count the number of letters in these expressions for "Thank You" from various languages and fill in the empty column in the table. Next, label the number line below the dot plot so that all of the data will fit. Finally, plot the data.

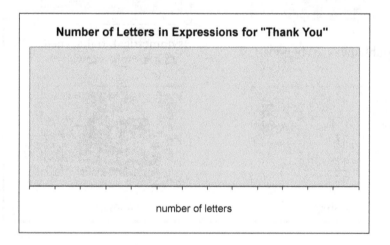

a. Describe the shape of the distribution.

b. Where is the peak of the distribution?

c. How many observations are there?

Language	Spelling	Number of letters
Afrikaans	dankee	
Arabic	shukran	
Chinese, Cantonese	do jeh	
Chinese, Mandarin	xie xie	
Czech	dêkuji	
Danish	tak	
English	thank you	
Finnish	kiitos	
French	merci	
German	danke	
Greek	efharisto	
Hawaiian	mahalo	
Hebrew	toda	
Hindi	sukria	
Italian	grazie	
Japanese	arigato	
Korean	kamsa hamnida	
Norwegian	takk	
Philippines (Tagalog)	salamat po	
Polish	dziekuje	
Portuguese	obrigado	
Russian	spasibo	
Spanish	gracias	
Sri Lanka (Sinhak)	istutiy	
Swahili	asante	
Swedish	tack	
Thai	khop khun krab	
Turkish	tesekkür ederim	
Vietnamese	ca'm on	

5. Make a dot plot from this data (winning times of a group of athletes for the 100-meter dash).

11.8   12.0   12.1   12.1   12.3   12.4   12.5   12.5   12.6   12.6   12.7
12.7   12.7   12.7   12.7   12.8   12.8   12.8   12.8   12.9   12.9   13.1

a. Describe the shape of the distribution.

b. Where is the peak of the distribution?

c. Describe the spread.

d. How many observations are there?

6. The graph shows the personal income of people in the United States, 15 years and older, in 2005. The graph does not show the approximately 13,000 people who earned more than $100,000. (The "k" in the chart means $1000. So, 50k means $50,000.)

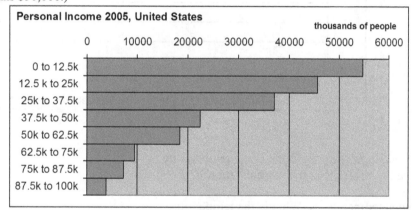

Source: Census.gov

This distribution does **not** have a central peak. If we turn it around, we can see the shape of its distribution: it is **J-shaped** (think of J that has been mirrored). The most common or "typical" values are NOT in the middle or center of the distribution, but instead fall into the first two columns (because the distribution is so asymmetrical).

a. Estimate from the graph about how many people earned less than $12,500.

b. Estimate from the graph about how many people earned between $12,500 and $25,000.

c. The total number of people who earned between $0 and $100,000 is 198,617,000. Now use your answer from (a). Approximately what *percentage* of people earned less than $12,500?

d. Use your answer from (b). Approximately what percentage of the people earned between $12,500 and $25,000?

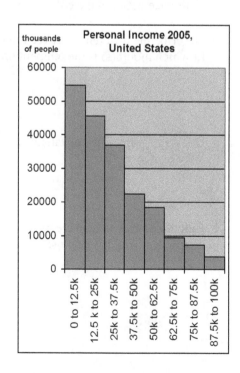

7. Line graphs are used to display information that changes *over time*. The line graph you will make below shows monthly average minimum and maximum temperatures for Dallas.

This is *not* a distribution because the data is not based on a statistical question. The question asked was, "What is the average minimum temperature in January? In February? ... " and so on, and similarly for the average maximum temperature. The answers to those questions do not vary: Over a number of years you record the temperature frequently, select for each day the maximum and minimum temperatures, calculate the monthly average of both for each month, and in each category you get a *single* answer.

a. Complete drawing the double-line graph using the data given in the table.

Month	Temperature Average	
	Min	**Max**
Jan	2	13
Feb	4	16
March	8	19
April	13	24
May	17	28
June	22	32
July	24	34
Aug	23	34
Sept	20	31
Oct	14	26
Nov	8	19
Dec	3	14

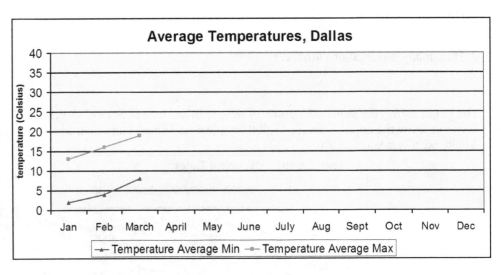

b. Look at the *maximum* temperatures. What is the temperature difference between the coldest and the warmest month?

c. Look at the *minimum* temperatures. What is the temperature difference between the coldest and the warmest month?

d. Describe the difference between maximum and minimum temperatures. In which month(s) is the temperature the greatest?

8. **a.** Does this graph show a statistical distribution? Why or why not?

b. Calculate what percentage of the candies are red and what percentage are green.

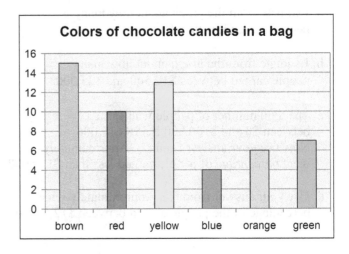

152

Mean, Median, and Mode

Mean, median, and **mode** are all measures for the *center* of a data set. In other words, each of them gives us a *single number* that (hopefully) indicates the "middle point" of the distribution.

<u>Mode</u> is the most commonly occurring data item within the data set.

- If no item occurs more often than others, there is no mode.
  For example, the data set *bear, parrot, cat, dog, lizard* has no mode.

- If two (or three, four, etc.) items occur equally often, there are that many modes.
  For example, the data set 3, 3, 6, 6, 7, 8, 8, 10 has three modes: 3, 6, and 8.

<u>Median</u> is the *middle* item after the data is organized from the least to the greatest. Exactly half of the data is before the median, and the other half is after.

- If there is an even number of data items, median is the average of the two items in the middle.

Example. Find the median of children's ages in a play group:
3, 3, 4, 6, 6, 7, 8, 8, **8**, **8**, 8, 9, 9, 9, 9, 10, 10, 10

There are 18 data items and they are already in order. The median will be the "midpoint", or the average of the 9th and 10th items, which are both 8. The median is 8. It matches well with the peak of the distribution.

What is the mode in this example?

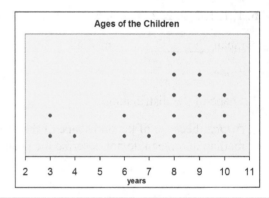

<u>Mean</u>, or the average, is calculated by adding all the data items, then dividing by the number of them.

Example. Mia's scores on her spelling tests were 80%, 72%, 88%, 92%, and 79%.

What was her average score?

We calculate the mean by adding the scores and dividing by 5: $\dfrac{80 + 72 + 88 + 92 + 79}{5} = 82.2\%$

1. Find the median and mode of these data sets.

a. 20, 25, 21, 30, 29, 24, 18, 32, 25, 26, 25 (ages of participants in a parenting class)

median _____   mode _____

b. 1, 1, 0, 2, 2, 2, 3, 1, 2, 2, 1 (the number of cars per household, for 11 households on Meadow Street)

median _____   mode _____

c. 80, 85, 80, 90, 70, 75, 90, 85, 100, 80 (Alice's quiz scores in algebra class)

median _____   mode _____

d. sandals, crocs, tennis shoes, crocs, dress shoes, sandals (types of shoes Emma keeps on her shoe rack)

mode _____

2. Joe practices swimming. These are the times it took him to swim 50 m free style, on six different days last week, given in seconds: 29.76 28.45 28.12 30.73 30.48 29.57. Find his average time.

3. Find the mean, median, and mode of the data sets. Draw a dot plot.

a. 4, 8, 2, 5, 5, 9, 3, 6, 5, 4, 4, 5, 1

mean _____ median _____

mode _____

Notice that all three measures are close to each other. This is not surprising, because this particular distribution is <u>bell-shaped</u> and has a very clear central peak.

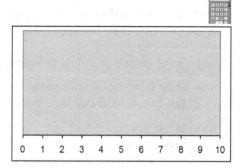

b. 1, 1, 1, 2, 2, 2, 2, 3, 3, 4, 6, 7, 7, 8, 8, 8, 9, 9, 9, 9, 9, 10, 10

mean _____ median _____

mode _____

Shape of the distribution: _____

Notice: because of the odd shape of the distribution, median and mean do not describe the peaks at all.

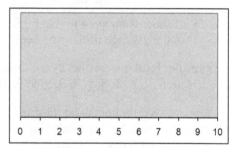

4. These are the grades a group of students got in a electronics course.

a. Make a bar graph from the data.

b. Find the mean, median, and mode.

mean _____ median _____ mode _____

c. Which measure(s) of center describe the data well?

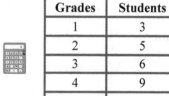

Grades	Students
1	3
2	5
3	6
4	9
5	4

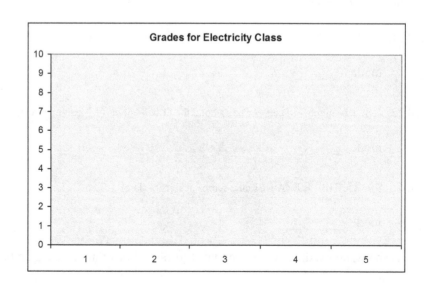

Grades for Electricity Class

Using Mean, Median, and Mode

Whether you use mean, median, or mode depends both

- on the **type of data** *and*
- on the **shape of distribution.**

Example. This distribution of science quiz scores is heavily skewed (asymmetrical), and its "peak" is at 6. Which of the three measures of center would best describe this distribution?

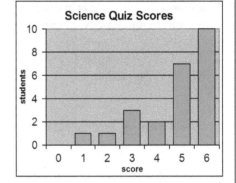

Let's calculate the mean, median, and mode.

Mode: We can see from the graph that the <u>mode is 6</u>.

Median: There are 24 students. The students' actual scores are 1, 2, 3, 3, 3, 4, 4, 5, 5, 5, 5, 5, 5, 5, 6, 6, 6, 6, 6, 6, 6, 6, 6, 6.

The median is the average of the 12th and 13th scores, which is <u>5</u>.

The mean is $\dfrac{1+2+3+3+3+4+4+7\times5+10\times6}{24} = 4.79167 \approx 4.79$.

Notice that the mean is less than 5, but the two highest bars on the graph are at 5 and 6. In this case, the mean does *not* describe the peak of the distribution very well because it actually falls outside the peak! Both the median and the mode do describe it well.

1. **a.** Find the mean, median, and mode of this data set: 3, 4, 4, 5, 5, 5, 5, 6, 8, 25.

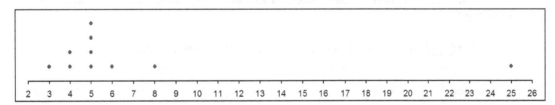

    mean _____ median _____ mode _____

b. Which of the three, mean, median, or mode, best describes the center of this data?

Clearly, either the _____ or the _____ , but *not* the _____!

The _____ is off from the central peak of the distribution.

The reason for this is that the data item "25" throws it off. This 25 is very different from the other data items in the set, and could even be a typing error! Such an item is called an **outlier**.

2. The graph shows the response to a certain question in a survey. It was measured as a *yes/no* question. Which of the below are possible to determine? (Mark with an "x").

_____ mean _____ median _____ mode

Hint: Imagine what the original data that was used to create the graph looks like.

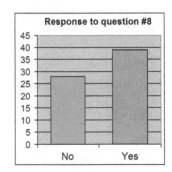

<table>
<tr>
<td>

Guidelines for using the mean, median, and mode

- The *mode* can be used with any type of data.
- The *median* can only be used if the data can be put in order.
- The *mean* can only be used if the data is numerical.

</td>
<td>

Sometimes, the median and the mean do not fall where the peak of the distribution is.

- The mean works best if the distribution is fairly close to a bell shape and does not have outliers.
- If the distribution is very skewed or has outliers, it is better to use median than mean.

</td>
</tr>
</table>

3. Judith asked 55 teenagers about how much money they spent to purchase Mother's Day gifts.

   a. Which of the numbers $11 and $9 is the mean? Which is the median?

   b. Would mean or median better describe this data? Why?

   c. *Approximately* what percentage of these teenagers spent $10 or less on a Mother's Day gift?

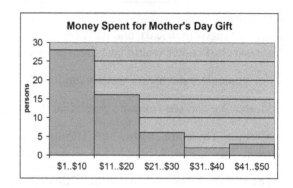

4. • Name what is being studied (usually the *title* of the graph tells you this).

   • Describe how the data was measured and in what units. For example, the respondents have given numerical answers in dollars. Or perhaps they chose either "yes" or "no."

   • Indicate whether the mean, median, or mode can be calculated. You do not have to find the mean, even when it is possible.

   Hint: Think <u>what kind of data</u> was used to create the graph (the original data).

<table>
<tr>
<td>

a. What is being measured or studied? _____

How is it measured?

Which are possible? (Mark with an "x").

____ mean ____ median ____ mode

The mode is: _____ The median is: _____

</td>
<td>

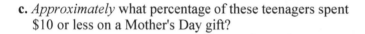

</td>
</tr>
<tr>
<td>

b. What is being measured or studied? _____

How is it measured?

Which are possible? (Mark with an "x").

____ mean ____ median ____ mode

The mode is: _____ The median is: _____

</td>
<td>

Eye Colors

</td>
</tr>
</table>

For the following data sets:

- Create a dot plot or a bar graph.
- Name your graph.
- Describe the shape of the distribution.

- Indicate how many observations there are.
- Choose measure(s) of center that describe the peak of the distribution, and calculate them.

5. **a.** The length of words on three pages in a children's storybook:

7 5 6 8 3 6 6 2 4 2 2 3 3 4 4 3 5 5 4
5 4 3 2 5 2 1 4 4 7 5 4 8 3 3 3 3 3 5
5 3 4 2 3 1 6 2 5 4 4 3 4 3 2 8

Here is the same data sorted:

1 1 2 2 2 2 2 2 2 2 3 3 3 3 3 3 3 3 3 3 3 3 3 4 4 4
4 4 4 4 4 4 4 5 5 5 5 5 5 5 5 6 6 6 6 7 7 8 8 8

b. A restaurant asked its customers some questions about their food and service. One question was, "How would you rate the meal you ate today?" There were five possible answers: "excellent," "good," "normal," "not so good," and "poor." The customers' responses are listed below:

normal   poor   excellent   good   good   excellent   good
normal   not so good   excellent   good   good   good
normal   normal   good   excellent   good   good good
not so good   not so good   excellent   good

Puzzle Corner   Can you find a quick, *mental math* method for calculating the mean for this data set?   102, 94, 99, 105, 96, 107, 101, 104 (the weights of a litter of kittens at birth, in grams)

Measures of Variation

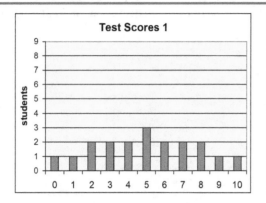

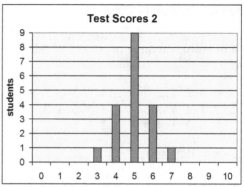

Look at the two graphs. The first gives the scores for test 1 and the second for test 2. *Both* sets of data have a mean of 5.0 and a median of 5. Yet the distributions are <u>very different</u>. If you were told just the mean and median, you would not know that!

How are they different? In test 1, the students got a wide range of different scores; the data is very scattered and **varies a lot**. In test 2, nearly all of the students got a score from 4 to 6. The data is concentrated, or *clustered*, around 5.

We have several ways of measuring the **variation** in a distribution.

One way is to use range. Simply put, **range is the difference between the largest and smallest data items.**

Example 1. For test 1, the smallest score is 0 and the largest is 10. The range is 10.
For test 2, the smallest score is 3 and the largest is 7. The range is 4. Clearly, the range is much smaller for test 2, indicating the data is clustered. The larger range of test 1 scores means the data is much more scattered.

Another measure of variation is the **interquartile range**.

To determine this measure, we first identify the **quartiles**, which are the **numbers that divide the data into quarters**. The **interquartile range is the difference between the first and third quartiles**. Since the quartiles divide the data into quarters, exactly half of it lies between the first and third quartiles. The smaller this measure is, the more concentrated the data is.

Example 2 shows how to determine the interquartile range.

Example 2. The scores for test 1 are: 0, 1, 2, 2, 3, 3, 4, 4, 5, 5, 5, 6, 6, 7, 7, 8, 8, 9, 10.
Find the interquartile range.

We need to divide the data into quarters. Finding the median naturally divides the data into two halves:

0, 1, 2, 2, 3, 3, 4, 4, 5, **5** , 5, 6, 6, 7, 7, 8, 8, 9, 10

Now we take *the lower half of the data,* excluding the median, and find *its median.* 0, 1, 2, 2, **3**, 3, 4, 4, 5. That is the **first quartile.**

Similarly, the *median of the upper half of the data* is the **third quartile**: 5, 6, 6, 7, **7**, 8, 8, 9, 10

The median itself is the **second quartile**.

Together, the three quartiles divide the data into quarters. The interquartile range is the difference between the third and first quartile, or in this case 7 − 3 = **4** .

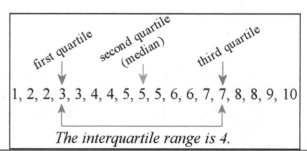

The interquartile range is 4.

1. Find the median and interquartile range of the data sets.

- First, find the median.
- Next, find the median of the lower half of the data (excluding the median itself).
- Then, find the median of the upper half of the data (excluding the median itself).

a. 5, 5, 6, 6, 7, 7, 7, 7, 7, 7, 8, 8, 8, 9, 10, 10

first quartile _____   median _____   third quartile _____   interquartile range _____

b. 2, 2, 3, 4, 5, 5, 5, 5, 6, 6, 6, 7, 7, 7, 9, 9

first quartile _____   median _____   third quartile _____   interquartile range _____

c. Let's say the data sets in (1a) and (1b) are the quiz scores of two groups of students.

Which group did better in general?

In which group did the quiz scores vary more?

Also, make bar graphs for the quiz scores of the two groups.

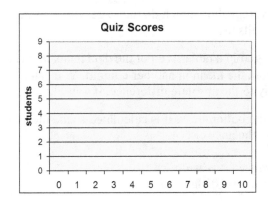
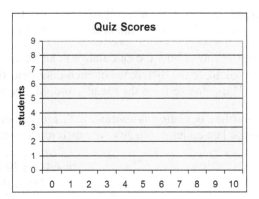

2. Find the range and the interquartile range of the data sets.

a. The number of paid vacation days in a year of the employees of a small firm:

6 8 10 10 11 11 12 12 12 13 13 14 14 14 15 17 18 20 24

range _____

1st quartile _____   median _____   3rd quartile _____

interquartile range _____

b. The heights of some children in centimeters:

136 138 139 139 140 140 140 140 140 141 141 141 142 144 144 145 147

range _____

1st quartile _____   median _____   3rd quartile _____

interquartile range _____

Mean absolute deviation

Yet another measure of variation is the **mean absolute deviation**. Use it only if you use the mean as your measure of center.

In a nutshell, mean absolute deviation measures *how much, on average, the various data items deviate (differ) from the mean*. In other words, for each data item, we calculate how much it differs from the mean, and then we calculate the average of those differences.

It is called "absolute" deviation because we use the absolute values of the differences from the mean. In other words, those differences are always taken to be positive, never negative.

It is easier to calculate mean absolute deviation using a computer because it involves so many calculations. Some calculators may also have it. Example 3 will make the process clear.

Example 3. Calculate the mean and the mean absolute deviation for the ages of people in a gymnastics group:

$$62 \quad 60 \quad 65 \quad 63 \quad 70 \quad 64 \quad 78 \quad 71 \quad 68 \quad 66 \quad 70$$

The mean is $\dfrac{62 + 60 + 65 + 63 + 70 + 64 + 78 + 71 + 68 + 66 + 70}{11} = 67.$

So the average age of the members is 67 years. On the average, how much do their ages *differ* from this mean of 67 years? That is what mean absolute deviation tells us.

The table below shows how the calculations can be arranged in a table. We put the data items in one column, and then we calculate the difference of each data item from the mean in another column. You can skip the column titled "difference from the mean", and go directly to the absolute difference, if you like.

The mean absolute deviation is abbreviated as *m.a.d.* in the bottom row. It is calculated as the mean of the numbers in the last column (the absolute differences) and the answer is 4.

	age	difference from the mean	absolute difference
	62	-5	5
	60	-7	7
	65	-2	2
	63	-4	4
	70	3	3
	64	-3	3
	78	11	11
	71	4	4
	68	1	1
	66	-1	1
	70	3	3
mean	67	*m.a.d.*	**4**

What does it mean to say that the mean absolute deviation is 4? It means that, on average, the member's ages differ from the mean of 67 years by 4 years.

Calculating mean absolute deviation using a spreadsheet program (Excel, LibreOffice Calc, *etc.*)

1.

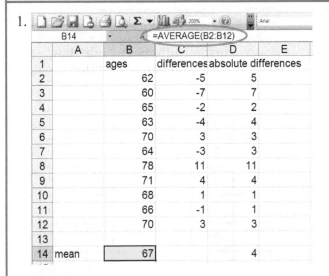

B14 — =AVERAGE(B2:B12)

	A	B	C	D	E
1		ages	differences	absolute differences	
2		62	-5	5	
3		60	-7	7	
4		65	-2	2	
5		63	-4	4	
6		70	3	3	
7		64	-3	3	
8		78	11	11	
9		71	4	4	
10		68	1	1	
11		66	-1	1	
12		70	3	3	
13					
14	mean	67		4	

To calculate the mean of a set of data, in the cell where you want the calculation to appear, type:

 =AVERAGE(B2:B12)

When you type the formula in the cell, it appears in the formula bar at the top, as in the image. A formula always starts with an equals sign.

Press "ENTER" to see the answer, 67.

2.

C2 — =B2-B14

	A	B	C	D	E
1		ages	differences	absolute differences	
2		62	-5	5	
3		60	-7	7	
4		65	-2	2	
5		63	-4	4	
6		70	3	3	
7		64	-3	3	
8		78	11	11	
9		71	4	4	
10		68	1	1	
11		66	-1	1	
12		70	3	3	
13					
14	mean	67		4	

Next we calculate the difference between each item of data and the mean.

Type "=B2 - B14" to subtract the values in cells B2 and B14.

The dollar signs in B14 make it an **absolute reference**, so it doesn't change when you copy and paste the formula into another cell. Pasting the formula into the cells below is a quick way to get the spreadsheet to calculate those values, too.

3.

D2 — =ABS(C2)

	A	B	C	D	E
1		ages	differences	absolute differences	
2		62	-5	5	
3		60	-7	7	
4		65	-2	2	
5		63	-4	4	
6		70	3	3	
7		64	-3	3	
8		78	11	11	
9		71	4	4	
10		68	1	1	
11		66	-1	1	
12		70	3	3	
13					
14	mean	67		4	

Now we calculate the absolute value of each difference.

In cell D2 type "=ABS(C2)" to calculate the absolute value of the number in cell C2. Then copy cell D2 and paste it into the cells below it to copy the formula and adjust the reference in it automatically.

4.

D14 — =AVERAGE(D2:D12)

	A	B	C	D	E
1		ages	differences	absolute differences	
2		62	-5	5	
3		60	-7	7	
4		65	-2	2	
5		63	-4	4	
6		70	3	3	
7		64	-3	3	
8		78	11	11	
9		71	4	4	
10		68	1	1	
11		66	-1	1	
12		70	3	3	
13					
14	mean	67		4	

Lastly, we are ready to calculate the mean absolute deviation by taking the average of the values in cells D2 to D12. In the cell where you want the value to appear, type "=AVERAGE(D2:D12)".

The answer "4" will then appear in the cell after you press "ENTER."

3. Calculate the mean and the mean absolute deviation for these sets of data. You can use a spreadsheet program on a computer if you have access to one.

a.

Art Club - members' ages			
	age	difference from mean	absolute difference
	7		
	9		
	9		
	10		
	12		
	13		
	13		
	13		
	14		
	14		
	15		
	15		
mean		*m.a.d.*	

b.

Prices of MP3 players			
	price	difference from mean	absolute difference
	29		
	30		
	33		
	34		
	34		
	35		
	35		
	35		
	36		
	36		
	37		
	39		
	42		
mean		*m.a.d.*	

4. Draw a dot plot for each data set in question 3.

a.

b.

5. For each data set above, answer the questions.

- What is the shape of the distribution?
- Based on the shape, which measure of center, mean or median, would better describe the data?
- Based on the best measure of center, which measure of variation should be chosen, interquartile range or mean absolute deviation?

Making Histograms

Histograms are like bar graphs, but the bars are drawn so they touch each other. Histograms are used only with numerical data.

Example. These are prices of hair dryers in three stores (in dollars). Make a histogram.

14 15 19 20 20 20 21 24 25 34 34 35 35 37 42 45 55

We need to decide how many bins to make and how "wide" they are. For that, we first calculate the **range**, or the difference between the greatest and smallest data item. It is $55 - 14 = 41$. Then we divide the range into equal parts (bins) to get the *approximate* bin width.

If we make five bins, we get $41 \div 5 = 8.2$ for the bin width. The bins would be 8.2 units apart. However, in this case it is nice to have bins that go by whole numbers, so we choose 9 for the bin width (rounding 8.2 up to 9).

The important part is that *all items of data need to be in one of the bins.* You may have to try out slightly different bin widths and starting points to see how it works. This time, starting the first bin at 13 makes the last bin to end at 57, which works, because the data will "fit" into the bins. (Starting at 14 would work, too.)

The **frequency** describes *how many items of data fall into that bin.* Lastly, all we need is to draw the histogram, remembering that the bars touch each other.

Price ($)	Frequency
13..21	7
22..30	2
31..39	5
40..48	2
49..57	1

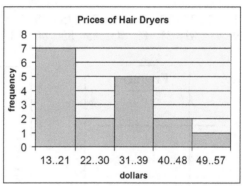

This is a **double-peaked** distribution and **skewed to the right** (the direction of skewness is where the "long tail" of the distribution is; in this case to the right). Since it definitely is *not* bell-shaped, the mean is *not* a good measure of center. Therefore, the *median* is the better choice for measure of center.

Consequently, we need to use *interquartile range*, and not mean absolute deviation, as a measure of variation.

The median is underlined below:

14 15 19 20 20 20 21 24 **_25_** 34 34 35 35 37 42 45 55

The 1st quartile is $20 and the 3rd quartile is $36 (verify those). So the interquartile range is $16.

This means that half of the data is found between 20 and 36 dollars. This price range is quite large for devices with a median price of only $25. A large range compared to the median describes data which is widely scattered. (We can also see that from the dot plot.)

Since the median is $25, which is nearer the low end of the interval from $20 to $36, the prices are somewhat more concentrated in the lower end of that interval.

For a comparison, look at the dot plot as well. It has a similar shape to the histogram.

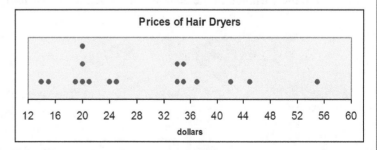

163

1. This data lists the heights of 24 swimmers in centimeters. Make a histogram with <u>five</u> bins.

155 155 156 157 158 159 159 160 162 162 163 163
164 165 166 167 167 168 168 170 172 174 175 177

Height (cm)	Frequency

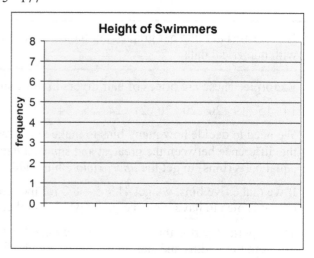

2. Make a histogram from this data, which lists all of the scores a basketball team had in the games in one season. Make six bins.

60 62 68 71 72 72 73 74 74 74 75 75 76 77 77 77
78 78 78 79 79 81 81 82 83 83 85 86 88 90 92 95

Score	Frequency

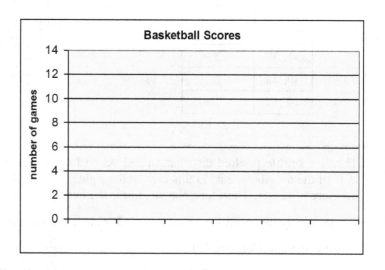

3. **a.** As this distribution has its peak near the center, you could use either mean or median as a measure of center. This time, find the median and the interquartile range.

median _____ interquartile range _____

b. Describe the variation in the data. Is it very scattered (varied), somewhat so, or not very much so?

4. Make a histogram from this data. Make five bins.

Country	Life expectancy at birth (years)
Chile	78.6
Uruguay	76.4
French Guiana	75.9
Argentina	75.3
Ecuador	75.0

Country	Life expectancy at birth (years)
Venezuela	73.7
Colombia	72.9
Brazil	72.4
Paraguay	71.8
Peru	71.4

Country	Life expectancy at birth (years)
Suriname	70.2
Trinidad and Tobago	69.8
Guyana	66.8
Bolivia	65.6

(source: United Nations)

Life expectancy (years)	Frequency

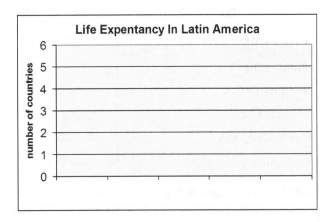

5. In a previous lesson you made a dot plot from this data (the winning times of a group of athletes for the 100-meter dash). This time, make two histograms, one with four bins and the other with five, and compare them. They look different! For a small data set, a dot plot or a stem-and-leaf plot may work better than a histogram.

11.8   12.0   12.1   12.1   12.3   12.4   12.5   12.5   12.6   12.6   12.7
12.7   12.7   12.7   12.7   12.8   12.8   12.8   12.8   12.9   12.9   13.1

a. Make a histogram with 4 bins.

Winning times (seconds)	Frequency

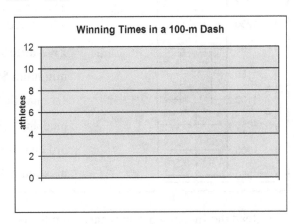

b. Make a histogram with 5 bins.

Winning times (seconds)	Frequency

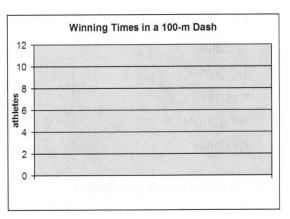

Boxplots

Boxplots or box-and-whisker plots are simple graphs on a number line that use a box with whiskers to visually show the quartiles of the data. Boxplots show us the **five-number summary** of the data: the minimum, the 1st quartile, the median, the 3rd quartile, and the maximum.

Example. We already looked at the prices (in dollars) of hair dryers in three stores.

14 15 19 20 20 20 21 24 25 34 34 35 35 37 42 45 55

Five-number summary:

minimum $14

1st quartile $20

median $24

3rd quartile $35

maximum $55

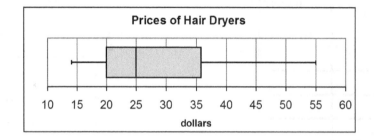

The box itself starts at the 1st quartile and ends at the 3rd quartile. Therefore, its width is the interquartile range. We draw a line in the box marking the median ($25).

The boxplot also has two whiskers. The first whisker starts at the minimum ($14) and goes to the first quartile. The other whisker is drawn from the third quartile to the maximum ($55).

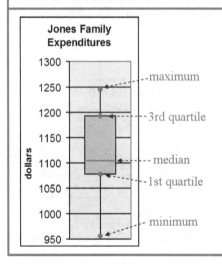

This boxplot shows the Jones' family monthly expenditures from 12 different months. This time the boxplot is drawn vertically.

The maximum expenditures (in some particular month) were a little over $1,250. The median is about $1,100.

Five-number summary:

minimum $956

1st quartile $1,077.50

median $1,105

3rd quartile $1,192.5

maximum $1,245

1. **a.** Read the five-number summary from the boxplot.

Five-number summary:

minimum

1st quartile

median

3rd quartile

maximum

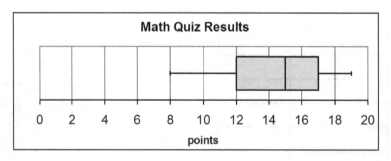

b. What is the interquartile range?

166

2. Make the five-number summary for the data sets, and draw a boxplot. Hint: For the boxplot, first draw a number line with an appropriate range.

---

a. the number of rainy days in August, in 20 different years

2 3 4 4 5 6 6 6 7 7 7 8 8 8 8 9 9 11 13 16

minimum

1st quartile

median

3rd quartile

maximum

---

b. prices (in dollars) of 1000-piece 3D puzzles

23 26 27 29 29 29 30 30 30 30 31 31 33 36 38

minimum

1st quartile

median

3rd quartile

maximum

---

c. science test scores for 7th grade class

46 55 58 60 62 64 65 66 66 68 70 70 71 72 72 73 75 78 81 82 85

minimum

1st quartile

median

3rd quartile

maximum

Boxplots are often used to compare two or more data sets. They provide an easy way to visually compare the middle points and the variability of the data (you can easily see the median, range, and the interquartile range).

If a part of the box or the whiskers is "short", the data in that part is concentrated compared to other parts. Or, if a part of a box or whisker is long, the data in that part is scattered.

3. Scientists gave three different groups of children some memory tests. The box plot shows the results.

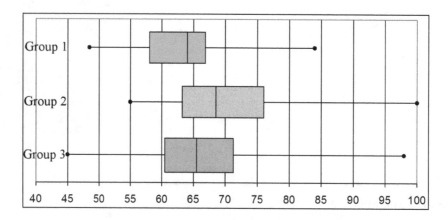

    a. Which group did best overall?

       How do you know?

    b. Which group varied most overall in their results?

       Which group varied the least?

       How do you know?

    c. Now look at the interquartile ranges. You can see them in the plots, because the box itself covers the interquartile range. Which data has the smallest interquartile range?

4. The following page lists the world's 25 tallest buildings and their heights. Your task is to choose a good graph for the data (the heights), and make it. Consider a dot plot, a boxplot, or a histogram.

\multicolumn{5}{	c	}{The tallest (completed and architecturally topped out) buildings in the world}
Rank	Building	City	Height (m)	Built
1	Burj Khalifa	Dubai	828 m	2010
2	Shanghai Tower	Shanghai	632 m	2014
3	Makkah Royal Clock Tower Hotel	Mecca	601 m	2012
4	One World Trade Center	New York City	541.3 m	2013
5	Taipei 101	Taipei	509 m	2004
6	Shanghai World Financial Center	Shanghai	492 m	2008
7	International Commerce Centre	Hong Kong	484 m	2010
8	Petronas Tower 1	Kuala Lumpur	452 m	1998
8	Petronas Tower 2	Kuala Lumpur	452 m	1998
10	Zifeng Tower	Nanjing	450 m	2010
11	Willis Tower (Formerly Sears Tower)	Chicago	442 m	1973
12	KK 100	Shenzhen	442 m	2011
13	Guangzhou International Finance Center	Guangzhou	440 m	2010
14	Marina 101	Dubai	432 m	2014
15	Trump International Hotel and Tower	Chicago	423 m	2009
16	Jin Mao Tower	Shanghai	421 m	1999
17	Princess Tower	Dubai	414 m	2012
18	Al Hamra Firdous Tower	Kuwait City	413 m	2011
19	2 International Finance Centre	Hong Kong	412 m	2003
20	23 Marina	Dubai	395 m	2012
21	CITIC Plaza	Guangzhou	391 m	1997
22	Shun Hing Square	Shenzhen	384 m	1996
23	Central Market Project	Abu Dhabi	381 m	2012
24	Empire State Building	New York City	381 m	1931
25	Elite Residence	Dubai	380.5 m	2012

Source: Wikipedia

Stem-and-Leaf Plots

A stem-and-leaf plot is made using the numbers in the data, and it looks a little bit like a histogram turned sideways.

In this plot, the tens digits of the individual numbers become the **stems**, and the ones digits become the **leaves**. For example, the second row 2 | 1 2 5 8 actually means 21, 22, 25, and 28. Notice how the leaves are listed in order from the smallest to the greatest.

Ages of the participants in the County Fair Karaoke Contest:
14 18 21 22 25 28 30 30
31 33 33 36 37 40 45 58

Stem	Leaf
1	4 8
2	1 2 5 8
3	0 0 1 3 3 6 7
4	0 5
5	8

4 | 5 means 45

Since stem-and-leaf plots show not only the *shape* of the distribution but also the individual values, they can be used to get a quick overview of the data. This distribution has a central peak and is somewhat skewed to the right.

You can also find the median fairly easily because you can follow the individual values from the smallest to the largest, and find the middle one.

Stem-and-leaf plots are most useful for data sets that have 15 to 100 individual data items.

---

1. **a.** Complete the stem-and-leaf plot for this data:

    19 20 34 25 21 34 14 20 37 35 20 24 35 15 45 42 55

    (prices of hair dryers in three stores)

    b. What is the median?

Stem	Leaf
1	
2	
3	
4	
5	

5 | 4 means 54

2. **a.** Complete the stem-and-leaf plot for this data. This time, the stem is the first two digits of the numbers, and the leaves are the last digits.

    709 700 725 719 750 740 757 745 786 770 728 755

    (monthly rent, in dollars, for one-bedroom apartments in Houston, Texas)

    b. Find the median monthly rent.

    c. Find the interquartile range.

    d. Describe the spread of the distribution (is the data spread out a lot, a medium amount, a little, *etc.*)

Stem	Leaf
70	
71	
72	
73	
74	
75	
76	
77	
78	
79	

71 | 9 means 719

3. The data below gives the average days with precipitation for cities in Texas. For example, the number 69 for Amarillo means that generally, the city of Amarillo gets at least some rain on 69 days out of 365 in a year.

a. Make a stem-and-leaf plot of the data.

City	Days with rain (average)	City	Days with rain (average)
Abilene	67	Houston	106
Amarillo	69	Lubbock	63
Austin	84	Midland-Odessa	52
Brownsville	73	Pt Arthur Beaumont	105
Corpus Christi	77	San Angelo	59
Dallas/Ft. Worth	79	San Antonio	82
Del Rio	63	Victoria	90
El Paso	49	Waco	79
Galveston	96	Wichita Falls	71

Stem | Leaf

b. Find the median and the interquartile range.

8 | 4 means 84

4. This stem-and-leaf plot shows the scores given to a gymnast in a contest by 10 different judges. Now the leaves are the first decimal digits of the numbers.

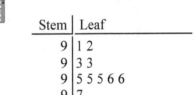

Stem | Leaf
9 | 1 2
9 | 3 3
9 | 5 5 5 6 6
9 | 7

9 | 7 means 9.7

a. What is the median of the scores?

b. What is the mean?

c. Which of the two measures of center describes the center of this distribution better?

5. a. Make a stem-and-leaf plot of this data.

254 248 232 255 250 227 235 238 260 231 259

(Results of a children's long-jump contest, in centimeters)

b. Describe the shape of the distribution.

Stem | Leaf

c. Which measure of center (mean, median, or mode) would best describe this data? Why?
(You do not have to calculate them, though you may.)

25 | 9 means 259

6. Make a stem-and-leaf plot of some data you gather. Then analyze your data. Include

- the number of observations
- how the data is measured (including the unit of measurement)
- the shape of the distribution
- the measure of center
- the measure of variability

Some ideas for gathering data:

⊕ Study the length of words in certain types of books or in one particular book.

⊕ Do a survey, asking a group of people about their height, age, or some other attribute.

Just remember that you need numerical data to make a stem-and-leaf plot, so asking for their favorite TV show or favorite color will not work here.

⊕ Study the volume of plastic containers in your kitchen cabinet (measure in milliliters).

⊕ Find some weather data on the Internet (with adult supervision).

⊕ Find prices of some gadget or item in a comparison shopping engine online (with adult supervision).

With your teacher's permission, you can also make some other type of graph (bar graph, histogram, boxplot) and analyze other types of data (non-numerical).

Mixed Review

1. Find the greatest common factor of the given number pairs.

   a. 87 and 36

   b. 96 and 16

2. Find the least common multiple of the given number pairs.

   a. 6 and 12

   b. 8 and 12

3. First, find the GCF of the numbers. Then factor the expressions using the GCF.

a. The GCF of 72 and 12 is _____ 12 + 72 = ____ (____ + ____)	**b.** The GCF of 42 and 66 is _____ 42 + 66 = ____ (____ + ____)

4. **a.** The points $(-8, 7)$, $(-5, 3)$, and $(4, 0)$
   are vertices of a triangle. Draw the triangle.

   b. Move the triangle five units down *and* three
   units to the right. Notice there are *two* movements!
   Write the coordinates of the moved vertices.

   $(-8, 7) \rightarrow ($ _____ , _____ $)$

   $(-5, 3) \rightarrow ($ _____ , _____ $)$

   $(4, 0) \rightarrow ($ _____ , _____ $)$

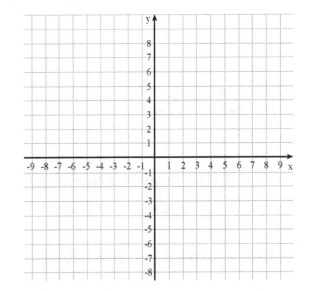

5. Write an equation for each situation—even though you could easily solve the problem without an equation!
   Lastly, *solve* the equation you wrote.

a. The area of a rectangle is 304 m^2 and one of its sides is 19 m. How long is the other side?
b. Mike weighed five identical books on the scales. They weighed 6.7 kg. What was the weight of one book?

6. Simplify the expressions.

a. $z \cdot z \cdot z \cdot 7$	**b.** $8 \cdot a \cdot 3 \cdot b \cdot 10$
c. $2 + x + x + x + x$	**d.** $5t - 2t + 6$

7. Add or subtract the fractions. Give your answer as a mixed number.

a. $\dfrac{5}{11} + \dfrac{1}{2} + \dfrac{5}{6}$
    b. $3\dfrac{11}{12} - \dfrac{5}{10} + \dfrac{1}{4}$

8. What part of a whole pizza is two-thirds of nine-tenths of a pizza?

9. A piglet is born weighing 3 lb 4 oz. If it gains approximately
   7 1/3 ounces per day during its 12-day nursing period, then
   how much will it weigh at weaning (the end of the nursing period)?

10. A string that is 5 3/4 inches long is cut into four equal pieces.
    How long are the pieces?

11. Simplify. In (e), write using a number.

   a. $|9|$ **b.** $|-3|$ **c.** $|0|$ **d.** $-(-28)$ **e.** the opposite of -7

12. Write an addition or subtraction sentence.

   a. You are at ⁻12. You jump 7 steps to the right. You end up at _____.

   b. You are at 2. You jump 8 steps to the left. You end up at _____.

13. On a separate sheet of paper, draw a right triangle with an *area* of 8 square inches.

14. Find the total area of the boat and its sail.

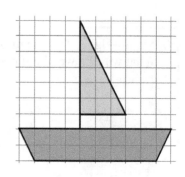

15. Find the area of the yellow shaded figure at the right.

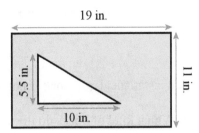

16. **a.** Name the three warmest and
    the three coldest months in Boston.

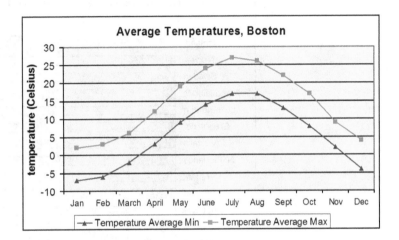

b. Now look at the maximum
temperatures. What is the
temperature difference between
the coldest and the warmest month?

c. About how much is the difference in maximum and minimum temperatures in August?

In January?

Puzzle Corner Be a teacher-detective: how did the children come up with these answers?

a. Jerry cannot figure out what went wrong:	**b.** Emily has something fishy going on here:
$\dfrac{2}{7} \div 1\dfrac{3}{4} = 6\dfrac{1}{8}$	$\dfrac{4}{5} \div 1\dfrac{1}{2} = 1\dfrac{3}{5}$
$2\dfrac{1}{3} \div \dfrac{2}{5} = \dfrac{6}{35}$	$2\dfrac{1}{3} \div \dfrac{1}{4} = 1\dfrac{1}{3}$
$1\dfrac{1}{5} \div 2\dfrac{2}{3} = 2\dfrac{2}{9}$	$1\dfrac{1}{5} \div 2\dfrac{2}{3} = \dfrac{3}{10}$
What error did Jerry make each time?	What error did Emily make each time?

175

Statistics Review

1. Is it a statistical question? If not, change the question so that it becomes a statistical question.

   a. Which kind of books do the visitors of this library like the best?

   b. How many pages are in the book *How to Solve It* by G. Polya?

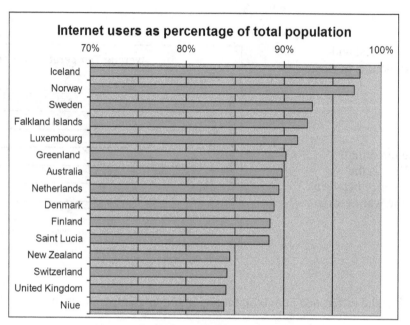

Source: InternetWorldStats.com

2. Fill in, using estimated percentages from the graph. In (c) and (d), round to the nearest tenth of a million.

   a. About _____% of the population of Norway use the Internet.

   b. About _____% of the population of United Kingdom use the Internet.

   c. The population of Netherlands was about 16,847,000 when these statistics were gathered (2011).

   So, there are about _____ million Internet users in Netherlands.

   d. The population of Finland was about 5,260,000 when these statistics were gathered (2011).

   So, there are about _____ million Internet users in Finland.

3. **a.** Find the mean, median, and mode.
   Hint: Recreate the list of the original data.

   Mean:

   Median:

   Mode:

   b. We notice this distribution has a *gap* at 5. What else can you say about the shape of the distribution?

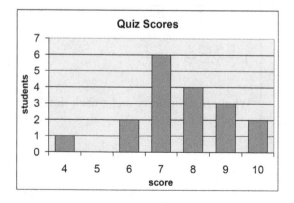

4. **a.** Find the five-number summary and the interquartile range of this data set, and make a boxplot.

   2, 5, 5, 6, 6, 7, 7, 7, 8, 8, 8, 9, 12

   minimum _____

   1st quartile _____

   median _____

   3rd quartile _____

   maximum _____

   interquartile range _____

   b. What could this data be?

5. **a.** Make a stem-and-leaf plot of this data.

   78 82 84 75 90 66 77 64 112 84 85

   (The heights of a group toddlers, in centimeters.)

   b. Find the median.

   c. Find the range.

   d. The data set has an outlier.
   Which number is the outlier?

   e. Describe the spread of the data.

Stem	Leaf

6. This graph shows the hourly wages in euros per hour of the 89 employees in the Inkypress Print Shop.

   a. About what fraction of the people earn 7-8 euros/hour?

   b. Describe the shape of the distribution.

   c. The mean is 9.66 euros/hour and the median is 8 euros/hour. Which is better in describing the majority's wages in this print shop?

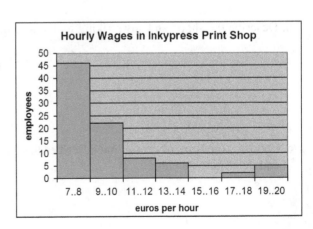

7. **a.** This data gives you the average number of days with precipitation in a year in 32 major European cities. For example, on average, in Amsterdam it rains (at least a little bit) 132 days out of every 365 days.

Create a histogram from this data. Make six bins.

Days with Rain	Frequency

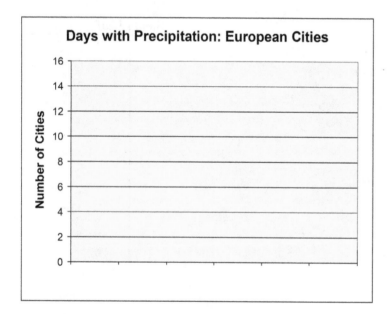

b. Describe the shape and any striking features of the distribution.

c. Choose a measure of centre that describes the data well, and determine its value.

City	Days of precipitation
Athens, Greece	43
Madrid, Spain	63
Bucharest, Romania	72
Lisbon, Portugal	77
Rome, Italy	78
Budapest, Hungary	81
Sofia, Bulgaria	81
İstanbul, Turkey	84
Warsaw, Poland	93
Prague, Czech Republic	94
Zagreb, Croatia	95
Tirana, Albania	98
Vienna, Austria	98
Kiev, Ukraine	99
Copenhagen, Denmark	102
Stockholm, Sweden	105
Berlin, Germany	106
London, United Kingdom	109
Paris, France	111
Oslo, Norway	113
Helsinki, Finland	115
Riga, Latvia	120
Moscow, Russia	121
Luxembourg, Luxembourg	122
Vilnius, Lithuania	122
Zurich, Switzerland	125
Tallinn, Estonia	127
Dublin, Ireland	129
Hamburg, Germany	129
Amsterdam, Netherlands	132
Reykjavík, Iceland	148
Brussels, Belgium	199

7. **d.** (Optional.) This data can also easily be plotted in a stem-and-leaf plot.
Make a stem-and-leaf plot and compare it visually to the histogram you made.

CPSIA information can be obtained
at www.ICGtesting.com
Printed in the USA
BVHW090747280620
582054BV00003B/8